£3.99
23 /100

D0849441

HENRY OF NAVARRE

By the same author

THE SCOURGE OF THE SWASTIKA
THOUGH THE HEAVENS FALL
THE KNIGHTS OF BUSHIDO
THAT REMINDS ME
IF I FORGET THEE
THE ROYAL CONSCIENCE
THE TRIAL OF ADOLF EICHMANN
THE TRAGEDY OF THE CONGO
SOUTH AFRICA TODAY – AND TOMORROW?
THE KNIGHT OF THE SWORD
DEADMAN'S HILL
CAROLINE THE UNHAPPY QUEEN
RETURN OF THE SWASTIKA?

LORD RUSSELL OF LIVERPOOL

Henry of Navarre

Henry IV of France

ILLUSTRATED AND WITH MAPS

ROBERT HALE · LONDON

Robert Hale & Company
63 Old Brompton Road,
London, S. W. 7.

PRINTED AND BOUND IN GREAT BRITAIN BY C. TINLING AND CO. LTD.,
LONDON AND PRESCOT

Contents

Illustrations

PICTURE CREDITS

Acknowledgements

I wish to express my thanks to the following:

To Monsieur de Laprade the Conservateur of the Château de Pau for giving me access to the archives, to the Directeur of the Bibliotheque Municipale in Pau for providing me with much useful information and to Madamoiselle Legrand for helping me with my researches in Pau.

For permission to quote extracts from their publications I am indebted to Albin Michel for *Henri IV, L'Homme* by Raymond Ritter; to the Bibliotheque Arniot—Dumont for *L'Etrange mort de Henri IV* by Philipps Erlanger, to Payot for *Henri IV* by Georges Slocombe; to the Librairie Artiènne Payard for *Henri IV* by Maurice Andrieux; and to the Librarie Hachette for Henri IV by Pierre de Vaissière.

My grateful thanks are also due to my wife who, in addition to typing the manuscript as usual, has had the difficult task of translating many of the original documents from sixteenth- and seventeenth-century French.

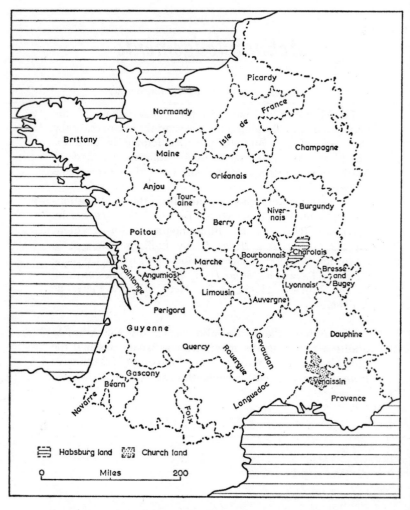

Provinces of France at the time of Henry of Navarre

Prologue

BEFORE the birth of Henry of Navarre, the first Bourbon King of France, Protestant beliefs had already swept through Germany, Switzerland, England, the Scandinavian Kingdoms, Scotland and Bohemia and had even penetrated into Italy and Spain.

In France the Reformation was not at first an open fight between the Catholic and Protestant faiths, and it was not until the reign of Francis I that it eventually developed into one. Nevertheless, even before Martin Luther, a German monk, nailed his ninety-five doctrinal theses on the door of the castle church in Württemberg, the French (or Gallican) Church was gradually becoming reformist, and many of the French bishops began a new teaching of the Bible which changed the face of Catholicism. They emphasized what to them seemed the only lesson to be learnt from the gospels, namely the "divine charity" of Christ, and deprecated the rites and liturgy of the Church of Rome, the invention of purgatory and the canonization of saints.

As early as 1508 a professor at the University of Paris, named Jacques Lefèvre, insisted that the original texts of the Gospels should be carefully studied. "It is because they have abandoned them," he said, "that the monasteries have wasted away, that piety is dead and that men prefer the good things of this world to those of Heaven."

For some years Lefèvre was held in high esteem, until the extreme views of Luther became generally known when he went so far as to call Rome Babylon and the Pope Antichrist. Until then many French Catholics had been in favour of reforming their Church but were not prepared for a break with Rome. Eventually, in 1520, Luther was excommunicated, and the same fate might well have befallen Lefèvre had he not received the protection of Francis I and his sister Marguerite, who was Henry IV's grandmother.

Francis, however, soon found himself in great difficulty. His sister, though herself a Catholic, had evangelical tendencies, whereas the French Parlement held very different views and when some of the inhabitants of Meaux smashed effigies of the Virgin and tore down public notices of papal indulgencies, which had been posted on the cathedral doors, they were tried by the Court of Parlement on charges of sacrilege, whipped and branded and some of them burned alive.

Some of his advisers urged the King to proclaim himself head of an independent Gallican Church divorced from Rome, and Henry VIII of England offered to support him should he decide to take such a step. He did not, however, do so.

From then on the situation worsened, and, as the extremists among the Protestants began to gain the upper hand in the movement, Francis became more orthodox. The walls of Paris were plastered with heretical posters and steps were taken to restore law and order. Those responsible were thrown into prison and their property confiscated. In 1545 two villages, Cabrières and Mérindol, both of them strongholds of extreme Protestant gangs, were, by order of Parlement, razed to the ground and many of the inhabitants burned at the stake; the others were banished from the realm. In Provence, by order of the Lieutenant-General governing the province, twenty villages were set on fire and their inhabitants massacred. In all 900 houses were destroyed and over 3,000 people killed.

With the death of Francis I in 1547 what had started as a peaceful movement to reform the Catholic Church gradually developed into open rebellion. The new King, Henry II, who was married to Catherine de Medici, was alarmed at the spread of Lutheranism, and two years after his accession set up a 'Burning Court' in the Parlement of Paris which had become the centre of the Protestant terrorists. This court was given the duty of bringing all heretics to justice, and informers were rewarded by receiving one-third of a convicted heretic's possessions. The penalty was death.

Meanwhile many influential and powerful recruits had been joining the ranks of the Protestants, including Admiral de Coligny and princes of the blood such as Navarre, Bourbon and

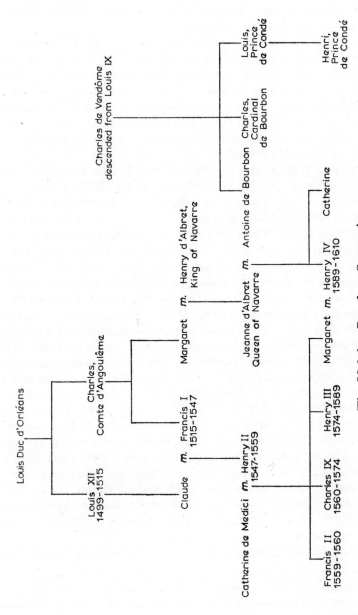

The Valois – Bourbon Succession

Condé, and in 1559 some of the Parlement judges openly declared that the existence of grave abuses in the Roman Catholic Church was indisputable.

All the Protestants now needed was a French Luther and a militant organization. It was not long before they got the former, Calvin the son of a lawyer in Noyon. He had left France in 1537, when to be a Protestant heretic was already becoming dangerous, and had settled in Geneva, to which city Luther had already fled after his excommunication. Geneva then became the main source of Huguenot propaganda which soon spread all over France.*

Even though Henry II, like his father Francis I, did not have the courage to proclaim himself head of the Gallican Church it would not have been too late after Henry II's premature death for such a step to be taken, and France might have been spared years of civil strife had the new king been made of sterner stuff. However, the last three Valois kings, as will be seen later, were the feeblest that ever sat on the throne of France. Francis II was a permanent invalid, Charles IX was a nervous wreck, and the last of them, Henry III was a degenerate. Their mother, Catherine de Medici, writing to the Queen of Spain, told her that God had left her with three small children and a wholly divided kingdom. Furthermore it seemed highly probable that none of them would provide any heir to the throne, in which event the Bourbons would become the ruling house. There were, however, two other contending families, the Guises, and the Montmorencys. The Guises had already given a queen to Scotland and a queen to France; Marie de Guise, who married James V of Scotland, and Mary Stuart, who married Francis II. The second of these two marriages gave them considerable power in France. Anne de Montmorency, who was High Constable of the Kingdom, was himself a Catholic, but he had three Huguenot nephews including the famous Admiral de Coligny. This meant that the Montmorency family had a foot in both camps.

The Guises, however, were fanatical Catholics. They were

* The Huguenots was the name given to the French Protestants by the Catholics. Historians over the centuries have made many suggestions as to how this name originated but to this day its real origin has not been authenticated.

the princes of Lorraine, and one of them, Francois, the Duc de Guise, was a national hero, famous for his defence of Metz against the Germans and the capture from the English in 1558 of Calais which they had held for 200 years. His brother, Charles, the Cardinal Archbishop of Rheims, would have been quite happy to have become the first head of an independent Gallican Church, but when it became evident that this was no longer a practical proposition he became one of the most fervent supporters of the papacy. Both Spain and the Vatican, therefore, henceforward regarded the Guises as the defenders of the Roman Catholic faith in France.

The two great leaders of the Huguenots were two Bourbon princes, Antoine de Bourbon, King of Navarre and the father of Henry IV, and his brother the Prince de Condé; neither of them could be regarded as die-hard Protestants but they were Huguenots. By that time the Huguenots were not merely religious reformers, and the Reformation had become a political party. Through the King of Navarre and the Prince de Condé the Huguenots gained great influence in the west and south-west of France and in Normandy, and this drew many of the lesser nobility and gentry of those regions into the conflict between Catholics and Protestants, which had by then become inevitable, for it was clear that the smallest incident might provoke a civil war. "The Huguenots by policy had joined forces with the Huguenots by religion and both were determined to get rid of the Guises".*

It was in 1562, two years after the death of Francis II, that the French Wars of Religion started and that the bitter feud between the Catholics and Protestants, which had been rumbling for many years, at last erupted like a volcano. For many years religious effigies had been destroyed, churches damaged or burned down, Catholic priests and Protestant preachers murdered. The last straw was the massacre at Vassy by the Guises' troops of a congregation who had been practising their Protestant cult in a barn.

Henry IV was then only 9 years old, but most of his life, and the whole of his reign, was to be spent in bringing peace to the kingdom and restoring it to prosperity after the ruination which it had suffered during the three religious wars.

* See *A History of France* by André Maurois.

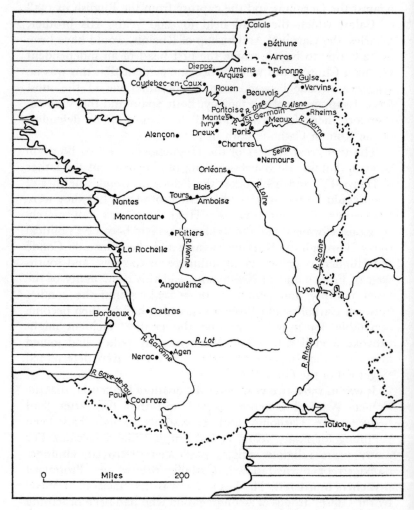

Main towns and rivers of France

1 His early years

Some are born great, some achieve greatness, and some have greatness thrust upon 'em.

Shakespeare *Twelfth Night*

IF the Valois dynasty had not come to an end in 1589 Henry IV would never have become the first Bourbon king of France. Nevertheless, he can rightly be said to have belonged to all of these three categories. Almost from the very moment of his birth he showed signs of being well above the ordinary child; he had greatness thrust upon him because he eventually became the rightful heir to the last of the Valois kings; and no one can say that he was not one of the ablest monarchs ever to sit on the throne of France.

He went through very difficult times in his early years and served a long and arduous apprenticeship, yet through it all he never lost his youth or his innate good humour, and he remained an incurable optimist – which was fortunate as it enabled him to overcome all the difficulties which lay ahead and which he took in his stride.

Even his birth was unusual. In the early hours of 13th December 1553, according to the story which has been handed down from one generation of Béarnais* to another, his mother, Jeanne d'Albret, who was in labour, was singing an old country song calling upon the Virgin of Jurançon to help her in her hour of travail. Before she had finished the baby boy arrived, without uttering a sound as is usual on such occasions, and this was taken as a sign that he was determined from the moment of his birth to enjoy life, which in fact he did, despite all the vicissitudes which he was to go through during the first two decades of his life. His mother was the only daughter of Henri

* The inhabitants of the province of Béarn.

d'Albret, King of Navarre, and the sister of Francis I. Her mother was always known as the 'Marguerite des Marguerites' and was often called the 'fourth of the Graces and the tenth of the Muses' for she was as gifted as she was beautiful. Jeanne was the spoilt child of Henri d'Albret and had previously been married to the old Duc de Cleves, a marriage which was subsequently annulled on the grounds of non-consummation. Before she eventually married Henry IV's father, Antoine de Bourbon, Duc de Vendome and Lieutenant-General of the Kingdom of France, she had refused the hand of the Duc Francois de Guise and the Infante of Spain, later to become King Philip III. Jeanne had inherited the exquisite charm of her mother but lost it long before she attained middle-age.

According to the legend her father was present during her confinement, and the moment his grandson made his entry into the world he seized him, rushed off with the baby in his arms to an adjoining room, there and then pushed a cup of wine under the boy's nose so that he could smell its 'bouquet' and rubbed his lips with garlic. Young Henry, so the story goes, showed no signs of displeasure and never uttered a sound; his grandfather was delighted.

The legend has since been embroidered, exaggerated and also deliberately falsified. It has even been suggested that what Henri d'Albret did was in the nature of a pagan baptism. A more likely explanation is that in the southern provinces of France, where the dreaded plague was rampant, the smell of wine and garlic was regarded as an effective antidote. The legend however, has been handed down by so many genera-tions of Béarnais that it cannot now be separated from history. Even those Frenchmen who know but little of Henry IV know the story of his birth.

Nevertheless, it was not the thought that perhaps he had saved his newly-born grandson from catching the plague which made him so delighted. He had another reason for happiness. He saw in the birth of the young prince an opportunity to restore the kingdom of Navarre to its former status. It had been dwindling for some years past, and by 1552 the provinces west of the Pyrenees had been lost. Henri d'Albret had always longed for such an opportunity ever since he had succeeded his father in 1516. He was determined to get his revenge on the Spaniards but so far had met with no success.

Henry IV might not have been born in Pau had it not been for the fact that his mother had decided to return there, leaving her husband in the north of France where she had been living a roving life with him, moving from camp to camp in Picardy, where he was in command of an army which was fighting against Charles V of Spain. The reason given for her sudden return to Pau was that her father wished the child to be born there and insisted on her making the journey immediately. There is reason to believe, however, that there was another reason for her decision, namely that she had heard a rumour that her father intended to marry a woman at court who had obtained some hold over him and to whom, Jeanne feared, he might leave most of his fortune. On her return to Pau, however, she was able to put an end to such a possibility and persuaded her father to make a will in her favour.

Hence another story – which, like the first, has the semblance of truth – according to which, after her baby had been delivered, her father handed her a gold box containing his will, although he himself kept the key. "This is for you", he is supposed to have said, and, taking the baby from his mother's arms, "This is for me". Exchange is no robbery.

Speaking later about the birth of a grandson who was to restore the kingdom of Navarre to its former glory, Henri d'Albret said, "See, my sheep has given birth to a lion." This was intended to be a riposte to the Spaniards, who had said offensively when Jeanne d'Albret had been born, "What a miracle, the cow has given birth to a sheep."*

The young 'lion', who was christened Henri de Bourbon and received the title of Prince de Viane, from the very beginning had a disturbed infancy. He was passed from one wet nurse to another, and although he did not have as many nurses as he was later to have mistresses he had more changes than can be good for a child.

At least eight of the wet nurses are known by name. The last of them was Jeanne Lafourcade, the wife of Jean Lassensaa, an agricultural labourer who lived in the village of Bilheres, as it was then called, and which is now part of Pau. The house

* The coat of arms of Navarre carried two golden cows *passantes*.

where he lived still exists, with the following inscription on the front door '*Saubegarde deei Rey*', (*Sauvegarde du Roi*). Later Henry IV gave his letters patent to Lassensaa in recognition of the devotion paid by him and his wife to the royal baby who spent his early months in the farmyards amongst all the animals.

By the time Henry was fully weaned his mother had left Pau. Antoine de Bourbon was once more in Picardy to resume his command in the campaign against Charles V of Spain, and his wife paid several visits to friends in France, including in her journey the Château de Fère en Tardenois in the Aisne, which had been built by her uncle Francis I. During their absence Henri d'Albret looked after his grandson just like a father and placed him under the charge of Suzanne de Bourbon-Busset, the wife of Jean d'Albret, Baron de Miossens, who lived in the Château de Coarraze in the village of Coarraze, which is situated in the valley of the Gave on the road from Pau to Lourdes.

It was there, according to the historian d'Aubigné, that the young prince was brought up like any ordinary Béarnais peasant, that is to say '*pieds et teste nue*'*, without any distinction from the other children of the district. He lived on the same diet; black bread, country soup, cheese and garlic; he played games with them and climbed the mountains with them. This, was exactly how his grandfather wanted him to be brought up, as he had no time for what he called the '*delicatesses francaises*', which were only suitable for the 'dolled-up playboys' to be found at the Court of Henry II. Above all, such an upbringing made a man of him and gave him a passion for country life and hunting which he retained all his life.

When Henri d'Albret died in May 1555 his daughter came back to Pau and, mindful of her father's wishes, continued to bring her son up in the same way as before. She did, however, take him away from Coarraze, and the next few years were spent mainly in Pau or at the Château de Nerac which always remained one of Henry's favourite residences. At the end of 1556 Antoine de Bourbon returned from Picardy to rejoin his family.

Doubtless owing to the influence of these early years, Henry always remained a man from the provinces, and this does not merely mean that he was a native of the Béarn. Many French

* bare-headed and bare-footed.

Kings were born in places other than the capital of France or its environments, but this had no effect whatsoever on what they were later to become, they were merely born away from Paris. But with Henry it was different. He was proud of being a Gascon and was not afraid of saying so for he regarded it as a compliment; and there was not a trace of snobbery in his character. Although he was a direct descendant of Louis IX (St Louis) he remained all his life not merely a country gentleman but a genuine man of the people, and, except for a brief stay in Paris, he spent practically the whole of the first fifteen years of his life in that part of France which lies between the Garonne and the Pyrenees, It was there that he made many friends amongst the *noblesse de province* who were for so long the backbone of France. The more refined atmosphere of Parisian court life never really appealed to him, and even when he paid his first visit to the Court of Henry II and saw the King for the first time he smiled sardonically at what he described as the 'fancy dress' that the King was wearing.

It was during this first visit that he had with Henry II a verbal skirmish, of which the following account has been handed down to posterity. The King apparently took an instant liking to young Henry, who was then not quite four years old. He thought that the boy was extremely good-looking and well-mannered and asked him whether he would like to be his son, to which the boy immediately answered, at the same time turning round and pointing to Antoine de Bourbon, "This is my father". "Well, in that case," the King said, "how would you like to be my son-in-law?" Without a moment's hesitation, and smiling broadly, the young prince promptly replied, "Oh, yes. I should like that very much," little knowing that fifteen years later he was to marry Marguerite de Valois, Henri's daughter.

On his return to Pau after his brief stay in Paris, Henry went back to Suzanne de Miossens at Coarraze, where he remained until 1560, when he returned to live with his parents in Pau and at the Château de Nerac. An unhappy period followed for he found himself embroiled in the constant rows which were the daily round in his parents' home and which, in a very short time, turned his mother, who until then had been renowned for her radiant smile, into a 'tight-lipped shrew'.

The cause of the trouble was religion and politics. Antoine de Bourbon, having married Jeanne d'Albret, who, since her father's death, had become Queen of Navarre, shared the throne with her. During the previous two decades the Reformation, which had swept through England and Germany like a hurricane, had begun to gain ground in France also.

Antoine de Bourbon, who had at first appeared to support the movement, for some reason or other suddenly changed his mind, returned to orthodoxy and was appointed Lieutenant-General of the Kingdom. Unfortunately, this recantation, though it cannot have been more than co-incidental, was accompanied by a complete change of moral attitude towards his marriage. He had previously been a loyal and faithful husband, but that now became a thing of the past, and even his own court were scandalized by his behaviour.

Whether it was due to a desire for vengeance, from conviction, or, as there is every reason to suppose, a combination of both, his Queen left no one in any doubt that she still embraced the Huguenot faith, and she continued to bring up her son as a Protestant.

After a time things became so unpleasant that she decided to go to Paris and take her son with her, in the hope that by removing him from his father's influence she would be able, as she wrote in a letter, "to rescue him from papism and debauchery".

From this moment young Henry was cruelly divided between his two parents. His mother refused to return to the Catholic Church, and, while he was staying at the Château St Germain with her, he performed a childish burlesque of Catholic ceremonies to the satisfaction and amusement of his mother. While they were staying at the court in Paris. however, Catherine de Medici* did everything she could to persuade Jeanne to give up the Huguenots. The more she tried, however, the more obstinately Jeanne resisted. The two women argued unceasingly about this, and on one occasion Jeanne d'Albret told the Queen Mother that if she held her son and the whole kingdom in her hands she would throw all into the sea rather than go to mass.

A year later, when Jeanne had been forced by her husband to return to Pau, leaving her son behind, Henry was made to

* The wife of Henry II.

renounce his heresy, and plans were set on foot to send him to the college of Navarre, famous for its Catholic religious teaching, where it was hoped he would be thoroughly indoctrinated with the Catholic faith. Before this could be done, however, his father died in 1562 of wounds received during the siege of Rouen, and at last the incessant fighting between his two parents and the misery which this caused was over.

After being wounded, it was a few weeks before Antoine died, but the Queen, although she received the news very quickly, did not bother to go to Rouen to look after him. The excuse given was that she had been told that his wounds were not regarded as serious and that he was making a good recovery. The real reason why she did not join him, however, was probably because one of her rivals, Antoine's mistress, Louise de la Béraudière, had got there first and was at his bedside when he died. What seems more inexcusable, however, was that she did not even go to Paris to join her son, who was still only nine years old, very upset by what had happened to his father and badly needed his mother's care and affection. In fact almost two years were to elapse before mother and son came together again.

There was, however, some justification for this, as the civil war in the Béarn had reached a rather critical stage, and Jeanne felt that it would be wrong for her to leave the kingdom until the situation became clearer.

The Catholics and the Protestant 'heretics' were fighting against each other in the Guyenne and Gascony as violently as they had been doing in northern France, and Monluc was threatening to invade the Béarn. However, many people who appreciate the reason for Jeanne d'Albret remaining in her province have, nevertheless, criticized her for not insisting that her son should leave the French court and join her. But there is a very good reason why she was also justified in deciding not to do this. It is thought to have been one of the conditions imposed upon her by Catherine de Medici for agreeing to give the Queen of Navarre some degree of moral support against the Guises, and young Henry had become the pawn in a veritable game of chess. Nevertheless, although he had to remain at Court his mother was allowed to issue strict orders with regard to his education, and this she did. She gave instructions that he

was to be brought up as a good Protestant, and they were faithfully carried out during the time he remained in Paris until
February 1567, when he finally returned to Pau.

He was by then thirteen years old. His early childhood had
certainly not been a happy one, but it had not destroyed his
natural gaiety or his *joie de vivre*. Already he had developed the
characteristics which were to distinguish him in later life. He
liked real men and had no time for weaklings. During the years
when he was brought up in Paris under the critical eyes of
Catherine de Medici she cannot have seen him growing up
without a feeling of disappointment and, perhaps, even of
envy, for her three sons, Francis, Charles and Henry, who were
to become three of the worst kings who ever sat on the throne of
France, could not hold a candle to him.

From the very moment when he set foot once again in his
beloved Pau he was subjected by his mother to the most rigor-
ous and merciless discipline. He was regularly beaten without
the slightest provocation, he was given very little to eat, he
slept on a wooden bed and was woken up almost at the crack of
dawn. He was sent all over Navarre and especially to the
mountainous country on fool's errands, particularly when the
weather was at its worst.

On one of these occasions his mother had told him that two
'*seigneurs*' had gone up a mountain track to fight a duel, and
that he must go at once and stop them. He immediately
mounted his horse and rode for miles in the direction in which
his mother had told him that the duellists had gone. Several
hours later he returned to the Château at Pau dripping with
rain and sweat and told the Queen that he could not find anybody. This kind of thing she did frequently, in order, she said,
to make him tough and hardy.

He was kept on the move without respite from dawn until
dusk, and if he still had any spare time left he had to spend it
saying his prayers. There was certainly much to pray for but
there were few or no grounds for thanksgiving. Nevertheless, he
took it all with great philosophy and never looked back on this
hard period of his life with any feeling of resentment.

In a letter which he wrote nearly forty years later to the
governess of his eldest son, the Dauphin (who was later to
become Louis XIII), he advised her to whip the boy whenever

he was obstinate.* He told her that when he was of the same age as his son he used to be beaten regularly and had benefited from it.

Whatever else this treatment did to him, it does not appear to have done him any harm. One of the leading magistrates writing about him during a visit which he made to Bordeaux said,

> "The Prince of Navarre is staying here. One must admit he is a nice person. At the age of fourteen he has all the qualities of a youth of eighteen or nineteen. He is at home with everybody and makes a great impression wherever he goes. He always says the right thing and never puts a foot wrong. He is undoubtedly a great Prince."

This was the opinion of all who met him, and the best proof of his advanced maturity was that women were already beginning to take an interest in him, which in any event was not surprising as he was physically quite attractive. He already had the long nose, a characteristic of many Béarnais, that was responsible for his nickname of '*Nez Long*'.

Meanwhile, during the twelve months immediately preceding the return of the young Prince to Pau, the Huguenots had improved their position considerably and had taken possession of forty towns. Hostilities were temporarily suspended in March 1568 by the Paix de Longumeau, but this precarious armistice lasted less than six months, by which time Admiral de Coligny and Jeanne d'Albret's brother-in-law, the Prince de Condé, had got together quite a large army based on La Rochelle. Catherine de Medici, realising the coming danger, was most anxious that Prince Henry should leave the Béarn and return to court, where he would be most useful as a hostage, and, should the Valois dynasty prematurely come to an end, as was not improbable, for her two remaining sons Charles IX and the future Henry III were both feeble creatures, he would then be the first Bourbon king, and, as he was still only fifteen years old, Catherine, who was drunk with power, would be Regent for at least a few years.

Having failed to lure him away from Pau with peaceful persuasion, she was forced to adopt other measures and plotted

* "*Opiniâtre*."

to have him kidnapped. Jeanne d'Albret described at length in her *Memoirs* what she called this criminal plot.

> The Queen Mother [she wrote] ordered de Losse, Seigneur de Banas to execute it. As he had been the Prince's tutor during the time Henry was in Paris it would be easy for him to gain access to his former pupil by giving some legitimate excuse for seeing him and then, having accomplished that, to get him away under false pretences while out hunting or, if this proved impossible, to kidnap him by force.

Fortunately the plot failed, de Losse never got as far as Pau, for, as the Queen of Navarre wrote, "he was stopped by the hand of God who struck him down with an attack of dysentery."

However, the Queen had been warned by a member of her own household that de Losse was on the way, and, even if he had arrived, she and her son would not have been there. She had already made up her mind, for this and other reasons, to leave Pau and go, via Nerac, to join Coligny and her brother-in-law Condé in La Rochelle. One of the main reasons was that she wanted her son to start fighting for the 'holy cause'.

Nevertheless, she had some doubts about leaving Pau, and, as she wrote in her *Memoirs*, she did not make the decision lightly.

When she arrived at Casteljaloux she was met by Monsieur de la Mothe-Fenelon, who had been sent by Charles IX to try and persuade her from joining up with 'those', and he was, of course, referring to Admiral de Coligny and the Prince de Condé, "who had so often brought about the ruin of his Kingdom and his house".

When, during the conversation which de la Mothe had with the Queen and her son at Casteljaloux, the young Prince was asked why he allowed his mother to get mixed up in all the 'troubles', he replied, to use the Queen's own words,

> that it was to save the pale of mourning because if one killed the princes of the blood one after the other the last of these would wear the mourning of the first and that dying together they would no longer have a kingdom. That was why he was going to see his uncle to live and die with him.

* The last of the religious wars was always referred to as '*les troisièmes troubles*', in the same way as the Irish rebellion of 1920 was known as 'The Troubles'.

I believe [the Queen continued] that de la Mothe said this to my son to show that the boy was so young and stupid as not to know exactly what he was doing.

On the following day, before de la Mothe left Casteljaloux, the Prince told him that he knew who was the spark who would set France on fire and he was not going to put it out with a bucket of water. De la Mothe, not understanding this reply, asked him why, to which Prince Henry replied that he would rather force the Cardinal de Lorraine to drink it until he burst.*

I have not told these stories about my son [wrote the Queen] to boast about him nor to be his historian but to make it clear to everyone that it was not out of stupidity, as so many people were saying, that he was taking this action. If at the age of fifteen, he was still an imbecile there could be little hope for his future. However, thank God, nobody thinks that of him now and it is evident that the zeal which it has pleased God to give him, his duty to his King and the friendship for his nearest relations are the three cords which brought him here.

His mother was quite right. Henry was no imbecile; he had a glib tongue and was never at a loss to say the right thing to suit the occasion. A typical example of this was given when he arrived with his mother at La Rochelle, where the magistrates were at the city gate to meet him and greeted him with an address of welcome, to which he made the following reply: "Gentlemen, my education has not been such that I can speak as well as you, but if my oratory is not up to the mark I will make up for it by my actions for I know much better how to act than to make speeches."

It was this natural buoyancy that was to stand him in such good stead during the next fateful two and a half years until an honourable peace was signed in August 1570 at St Germain en Laye. It enabled him during those years to accept defeat and disaster without flinching, to survive the assassination of his uncle, the Prince de Condé, in 1569, the defeat of the Huguenots at Poitiers and their retreat through the Languedoc.

* The Cardinal was one of the two Guises, his brother Francois was a soldier, but he was the representative of fanatical and intransigeant Catholicism. He was the real leader and was described as a Dictator, Pope and King. The Guises were one of the three families struggling for control just after the accession of Francis II to the throne of France.

Nevertheless, he was not yet old enough to be given even a nominal command of the Huguenot forces, although his uncle was prepared to hand over command to him as he was the senior prince of the blood and head of the leading branch of the Bourbon family. His mother very sensibly refused to entertain the idea, while making it clear that he would take over command as soon as he was old enough. When, however, she presented him with his first suit of armour, which she did in front of the troops on a special parade, she said, "All Europe has its eyes on you. You are no longer a child. Go and learn under Condé to be a commander."

From the moment of the arrival of the Queen and her son in La Rochelle the civil war continued with appalling barbarity on both sides. Catholics and Protestants both committed appalling atrocities, some to satisfy their hatred, others merely as an excuse for looting and pillage. In Paris the Catholic mobs set fire to Protestant houses and the Protestants burned Catholic churches. After a time both sides enlisted mercenaries to fight for them, the Catholics from Spain and the Protestants from Switzerland and Germany. Fighting on either side were sometimes members of the same family. As Le Noue wrote:

> each man reflected in his own heart that those whom he saw advancing towards him were Frenchmen among whom were probably some who were his relations or friends and within an hour they would have to kill each other. This made the event something horrible.

Monluc in his *Commentaries* – and there is documentary evidence to support his statements – wrote that the Huguenots massacred all and sundry, raped women and young girls and, after eating all the food they could find in the towns and villages which they had occupied, set fire to churches, monasteries and farms. They took everybody prisoner, including poor peasants and their children, kept them prisoner in terrible conditions, strung them up with yokes around their necks in order to make them hand over their gold and silver and burned the soles of their feet until they gave up all their possessions.

All this was done by people who were fighting each other merely because they worshipped the same God in a different way.

Prince Henry saw all this with his own eyes, and it must have created an unforgettable impression on him, for later, when the Huguenot troops were in Agen, he issued orders to the effect that trade and farming must be allowed to continue unmolested, and he made the officers commanding the troops personally responsible for their conduct and punished severely rape, arson and looting. All these atrocities which he witnessed during those early years had the effect of impressing upon him the importance of order, discipline and authority which were, first and foremost, the characteristics of this future king.

By 1570 both sides in this internecine campaign were ready for at least a temporary cessation of hostilities, even if a real peace could not be obtained. A Huguenot victory at Arnay-le-Duc, after a series of defeats made this possible and a treaty was signed at St Germain-en-Laye in August 1570. It gave the Protestants throughout the Kingdom 'liberty of conscience' and the right to practice their religion openly wherever they had exercised it prior to the outbreak of war. It also conceded to the Calvinists four towns: La Rochelle, Montauban, La-Charité-sur-Loire and Cognac. Furthermore, Charles IX formally recognized the Queen of Navarre and her son as 'loyal relations' and extended the hand of friendship to all those, even including princes of other countries, who had fought on the side of the Huguenots.

The peace, though perhaps it would be more accurate to call it an armistice, was to last for six years, except for a brief interlude during the siege of La Rochelle, and during that time Henry was to be its hostage as well as its guardian. Jeanne d'Albret herself from the outset had reservations about it, but it was not until after the massacre on St Bartholomew's Day that the Protesants in general saw it as a snare which had been set to lull their suspicions of the Catholics' future plans to destroy them.

2 A marriage of convenience

FOR a time there was a period of *rapprochement* between Catherine de Medici and her former enemies. Admiral de Coligny had managed to win the King's confidence, but Jeanne d'Albret and her son had meanwhile, returned to the Béarn to get some rest after the strenuous last few months and at the same time to restore order in the Kingdom of Navarre.

Catherine, however, did not intend to leave them alone, and she remembered the occasion when her husband, Henry II, had asked Prince Henry whether he would like to marry Marguerite de Valois and the reply which was given.

There had been another plan on foot, namely to try and bring about a marriage between the Duc d'Anjou, later to become Henry III, and Queen Elizabeth of England. His mother was against such a marriage. The real reason for her opposition was that she was afraid that the Duc d'Anjou, who was her favourite son, although he once referred to her as "*La Serpente*" might lose the succession if he were no longer in France when Charles IX died, as the astrologers had predicted he shortly would, and this would mean the end of the Valois dynasty and of her being the power behind the throne.* The reason which Catherine gave publicly was that it was rumoured that the morals of '*La Vierge d'Albion*', as she called Elizabeth, were not all that they should be.

Nor was this all. She had recently heard that Admiral de Coligny was anxious that Henry of Navarre should marry Elizabeth, and Catherine saw in this a great danger, as an alliance between the English and the French Protestants might

---

* She had apparently got over this fear within the next two years when she put the Duc d'Anjou up as candidate for election as the King of Poland in July 1572 when the throne became vacant.

prove extremely formidable, and Elizabeth had already helped and encouraged the Huguenots, as Philip II of Spain had the Catholics.

These were two of the reasons for Catherine's decision to offer the hand of her daughter in marriage to Henry of Navarre, whom she realised might one day become the heir presumptive to the throne of France. But there was a third. Her daughter Marguerite was in love with the young Duc de Guise and they had become secretly engaged. Such a marriage might have brought about most serious political complications and had to be avoided at all costs. Fortunately her son Charles was all in favour of a marriage with Henry, and Admiral de Coligny was easily won over. Jeanne d'Albret, however, needed more persuasion. The long negotiations began in the autumn of 1570 and continued for eighteen months.

Henry himself had never been madly keen on the idea, and he left Charles in no doubt about his feelings, but eventually both he and his mother had to give way. It was not only due to the pressure which de Coligny brought to bear on them. Many of their Huguenot subjects and followers felt that such a marriage might help to bring about a more permanent and stable reconciliation between the Catholics and the Protestants.

Accordingly, Jeanne d'Albret, early in March 1572 went up to Blois, where the court was then in residence, to continue the negotiations and found to her dismay that they had already reached the point of no return. All she could do, therefore, was to insist on a compromise with regard to the marriage ceremony.

She had tried to insist as a condition of marriage that Marguerite de Valois should leave the Catholic Church and be converted to Calvinism. It was finally agreed, however, that the bride would not change her religion nor would Henry attend mass on the day of the wedding. The marriage would not be solemnized in Church, and Cardinal de Bourbon would pronounce the couple man and wife, not as a priest but as uncle of the bridegroom. Furthermore, it was agreed that the Pope should be asked to grant a dispensation for this mixed marriage, but that if he were to refuse the marriage would still take place. Full agreement was reached on 4th April and on the following day the Queen of Navarre wrote to the Queen of England to give her the good news.

Madame,

Yesterday a final decision was arrived at for the marriage of Madame with my son.

Since my arrival in Blois, fortunately, although the Devil has done his best to prevent it, through God's intervention those who were in favour of union and peace won the day.

Jeanne d'Albret.

On 11th April the marriage contract was duly signed. The king agreed to settle a '*dot*' of 300,000 écus on his sister, and she was given 200,000 livres by her mother as a wedding present.

Although Henry was then eighteen years old and precocious for his age, his mother still regarded him in some ways, as a boy as the following letter proves:

My son, being sorry to hear about your illness I send this letter by hand and ask you to send me a reply by return. Madame* fusses so much over me and the food is so good that I hope that this will please you. I ask you to do these things, to behave like a gentleman, to speak boldly and even in places where you might be taken aside because what you say will be taken note of and even printed hereafter. Get used to combing your hair up but not in the old fashioned way. I advise this because I prefer it. What I would also like is that you should oppose any attempts which may be made to debauch you either in your life or your religion, to make yourself invincible to all this because I know that this will be their aim. The King will soon be getting in touch with you to hear your news. One can hardly believe how much you stand for at the Court here. As for Me, I believe that you are held in the same esteem as Monsieur le Duc.†

I am writing the rest of my news to Mr Beauvoir who will tell you all about it so I end this letter praying God to give you his holy blessing.   From your good mother and best friend.
Blois, 25 April 1572.

Shortly after this letter was written, Charles IX asked the Queen of Navarre to travel up to Paris from Blois and help with the arrangements for the wedding. She did so and spent a very busy three weeks buying all the necessary things. She had not been in good health for some time and was worn out with the strain of the last three months which had been considerable. On

* Catherine de Medici.
† The Duc d'Anjou.

Henry of Navarre, Henry IV of France

Mother and father of Henry of Navarre, Antoine de Bourbon
and Jeanne d'Albret

The Château de Pau, birthplace of Henry of Navarre

5th June she was confined to bed with a violent fever, and four days later she died. She never lost consciousness during her short illness, but she seemed certain from the moment when she first fell ill that she was going to die.

The suddenness of her illness started a crop of rumours that she had been poisoned, perhaps not altogether surprising remembering the fact that she had been, since her arrival in Blois, the guest of Catherine de Medici. What tourist visiting the Château at Blois has not been shown her special powder closet with the cupboards in which she used to keep her poisons.

The favourite story was that the Queen of Navarre had been poisoned by the smell of some gloves and collars sold to her by a perfume merchant named René, who had come to France from Florence with Catherine and was supposed to hold the equivalent of what would be called in England, if such a thing existed, Her Majesty's Royal Warrant for poisons. Another story was that she had eaten poisoned food when having supper with the Duc d'Anjou. But, although many generations of Huguenot historians have continued, without any evidence but for obvious reasons, to suggest that Jeanne d'Albert was poisoned, neither Admiral de Coligny nor the Prince de Condé nor even her own physician Caillard ever questioned the fact that her death was due to natural causes.

Unfortunately all this happened so suddenly that Henry was not with his mother when she died nor was he able to get to Paris in time for the funeral which was held quickly with a complete absence of pomp or ceremony.

At the urgent request of his future brother-in-law, the reigning monarch Charles IX, who wanted him to get to Paris as soon as possible once the marriage contract had been signed, Henry had left for Paris just a fortnight before his mother was taken ill; but he was in no hurry and stopped on the way to spend two or three nights at his beloved Château at Nerac. Once there, he decided to stay a little longer, in order, so the story goes, to carry on a flirtation with Fleurette, the gardener's daughter, who was most attractive and was supposed to have a soft spot for him. How little truth there is in the story, which was elaborated as it went the round of the gossips, can be judged from the following: after Henry had left Nerac for Paris, it was said, Fleurette was so upset that she drowned herself in the fountain of St Jean, situated in the lovely woods full of beeches in the *château* grounds, whereas, in fact she was still alive and flourishing twenty years later, by which time she had succeeded her father as gardener to the King, who was then Henry himself.

It was only when Henry arrived at Chaunay, in the Poitou, that the news of his mother's death reached him, but instead of pressing on, as might have been expected, it was not until three weeks later that he eventually reached Paris. He was of course, now the King of Navarre.

Various explanations have been given for his delay, including a suggestion that some of the Huguenot leaders were afraid that once he was in Paris he would be caught like a rat in a trap and that this was why Charles IX, urged on by Catherine de Medici, wanted to get him there, high and dry, as quickly as possible. Others, however – and Admiral de Coligny was one of them – insisted that he should honour the marriage contract which his mother had negotiated after so much trouble. So on the 7th July, accompanied by the Prince de Condé and 900 noblemen from Gascony, Henry entered Paris.

It certainly seemed from the reception which greeted him when he arrived at the Louvre that Coligny had been right and the opposing faction wrong. The Queen Mother welcomed him with open arms, and Charles IX went out of his way to disarm the Huguenots who had accompanied their new king of any suspicions which they may have entertained about his safety – suspicions which were, however, soon to be proved more than justified. Before seven weeks had passed the massacre of St Batholomew had taken place.

From the moment he arrived in Paris until 1576, when he decided to go back to Nerac, he became, as one of his French biographers has described it, 'the surety and the hostage' of the peace established by the signing of the Treaty of St Germain-en-Laye.*

On 17th August 1572, at a reception given at the Louvre by Charles IX and the Queen Mother, the official announcement of the marriage was made, and on the following day the ceremony took place. As the bridegroom persistently refused to abjure the Protestant faith and become a Catholic the cere-

* *Le gage et l'otage de la paix.* See *Henry IV* by Pierre Vaissiere.

mony was performed by the Cardinal de Bourbon on a large dais which had been erected in front of the west door of Notre Dame. When the moment came for her to give her verbal consent to become Henry's wife she gave an obvious sign of disapproval and, as she did so, gazed in the direction of another Henry, the Duc de Guise, with whom she was really in love and who was standing only a few feet away. A similar incident was to take place some 250 years later at the marriage in Westminster Abbey of George IV and Caroline, although on that occasion it was the bridegroom and not the bride who gave visible signs of displeasure.**

Marguerite de Valois's brother, Charles IX, was, however, standing beside her and lost no time in dealing with the situation. He quickly put his hand on the back of her neck and pushed her head downwards, which the Cardinal accepted with considerable relief as an indication of the bride's assent.

Henry and Marguerite being now pronounced man and wife, the bride left the dais and entered the Cathedral, where mass was sung. Her bridegroom, together with his escort of Huguenot *seigneurs* only accompanied her as far as the choir, where he left her and went to the archbishop's cloister to wait for the bride to leave the cathedral when mass was over. When she reappeared Henry kissed her, while Charles looked on with an ironic smile on his face. The festivities which followed the marriage ceremony went on for four days and included a ball at the Palais du Louvre, theatrical performances and a strange symbolic masquerade depicting a kind of epic conflict between the Catholics and the Huguenots, which left the object of the performance in no possible doubt. The roles of the two principal Catholics were played by Charles IX and his brother, while those of the Protestants were taken by Henry of Navarre and some of the Protestant Princes who appeared as fallen angels kicked out of Heaven and thrown into Hell. They were only saved from this fate by the intervention of Cupid and a troop of nymphs, among whom was Marguerite de Valois, who danced in a ballet with the King of France and the Duc de Guise. This offensive allegory was crystal clear to all who were present. The King of France had relegated the Hugenots to Hell from

** See "Caroline, the Unhappy Queen" by Lord Russell of Liverpool, (Robert Hale, 1967).

which they escaped by the intervention of love. The whole performance was a strange and ominous prelude to the bloody massacre of St Bartholomew which was to take place only three days later.

Despite the Treaty of St Germain-en-Laye the ill-feeling between Catholic and Protestant had never been more acute, and the last few days had done nothing to appease it. The Protestants were appalled at the attitude of the French Court, which could not have been in poorer taste; as for the Catholics, they objected to the incursion of so many Huguenots, and this had made matters worse. On the very next day Coligny was wounded by a gunshot which severed the first finger of his left hand and entered the arm. "That is how they treat a man who has nothing but good intentions," he said, and pointed to the window through which the shot had been fired. He had, in fact, identified his would-be murderer who was none other than a member of the Duc de Guise's suite, a man named Maurevert. The house from which the shot had been fired belonged to the Duc de Guise, and the horse on which Maurevert had made good his escape came from Guise's stable. There could be little if any doubt that the Guises were responsible for the attempt on Admiral de Coligny's life, and there was every reason to believe that the Queen Mother was also behind it.

The marriage of the King of Navarre and Marguerite de Valois could not have begun in more inauspicious circumstances.

Charles IX, however, was furious at what had happened. "Will they never leave me in peace?" he said when he heard the news on returning to the Louvre after a game of tennis.

In the Louvre itself there was much consternation. The gravity of the situation was realized by everybody, and the repercussions which the attempt to murder Coligny would probably set on foot were fully realized. As soon as the Huguenots heard what had happened they rushed into the streets threatening to kill the Guises. The same afternoon the King of France and the Queen Mother paid a visit to the Admiral at his bedside, expressing their regret and promised him that they would bring the criminal to justice, a promise which the King repeated the same evening to all the foreign ambassadors accredited to the French court, whom he had summoned to the

Louvre for that purpose. Meanwhile, the King of Navarre and the Prince de Condé had signed a proclamation protesting against the attempt on Coligny's life and promising swift vengeance. The atmosphere in Paris that night was explosive; no one knew what would be the outcome but many feared the worst – and well they might.

Alarming rumours became the order of the day. Some said that the Guises were going to attack the Protestants and others that the Protestants were going to kill the Guises. Paris was in a feverish state and dangerously excited. Thunder filled the air, and all Parisians were waiting for the lightning to strike. Catherine de Medici was afraid that the Huguenots, believing that the King of France was really responsible for the attempt on Admiral Coligny's life, might stage a *coup d'état* against the monarchy or that perhaps the Guises would start a Catholic uprising against the King and form a rival government, thereby killing two birds with one stone and satisfying their two main objects in life: the end of Protestantism and the substitution of the Guises as the royal family of France in place of the House of Valois.

Meanwhile, the Guises were not wasting any time. With the assistance of a former Provost*, a goldsmith named Claude Marcel, and a band of monks, they warned the Parisians to be ready for trouble and distributed guns, halberds and armour to as many as possible. By the morning of 23rd August the whole of Paris was ready for the fray.

As a result of the religious wars, the economy of France was in a pitiful state, and nowhere was this more apparent than in large cities, particularly in the capital. The common people disliked the Huguenots, not solely because of their religion but also because many of them were wealthy merchants. They were regarded as aristocrats of wealth and hated more than the real aristocracy itself. Money was scarce, prices high. A massacre of the Huguenots would be a form of revolution and much more likely to be successful than an uprising against the Government, as they would have on their side, all the Catholics who were loyal to the Crown; and Paris was ready for any kind of revolution. As dusk fell it was clear that anything could happen on the morrow.

* The Mayor of Paris.

By now the Huguenots were well aware that something was going to happen, but they were in such a state of panic that they could not think clearly. Some of them wanted to flee from Paris and take the Admiral with them, others wanted to warn the King and ask for royal protection, some of them even threatened the life of the Queen Mother, whom nobody really trusted. Ever since the death of her eldest son, Francis II, which left his younger brother Charles, a sickly child, on the throne, Catherine had been in command, the power behind the throne. The Bourbons and the Guises were the two principal contenders for the monarchy should the Valois dynasty come to an end. She therefore decided to walk the tightrope between these two rival families and alternately threatened the Bourbons with the Guises and the Guises with the Bourbons. In order to keep this political balance it was obviously necessary to have the Queen of Navarre on her side. It was, indeed, a strange relationship but it worked because it suited them both. No one knew precisely which way Catherine would jump, but everybody was convinced that she would only do what she felt certain would be in the best interests of her 'blue-eyed boy' the present King.

There was one thing of which the Huguenots were quite sure: that Coligny's life was now more than ever in danger and they asked the King to ensure that the Admiral's house was properly guarded, which Charles agreed to have done. The arrangements were, however, left to his brother, the Duc d'Anjou, to carry out, and he took care to see that a personal enemy of Coligny, a man named Cosseins, was put in charge of the guard of French and Swiss who were detailed for this purpose.

It was midnight, 23rd August 1572, the eve of St. Bartholomew's day, and Admiral de Coligny had just gone to bed. In the adjoining room were three of his intimate friends, including Pastor Merlin and a German named Nicolas Muss. At the foot of the staircase were a number of the King of Navarre's Swiss bodyguard, and outside the front door was Cosseins with his guard of fifty men. About 4 a.m. Henri de Guise, his uncle the Duc d'Aumale and the "*Batard* d'Angouleme"* clattered into

* The Bastard of Angoulême was the name by which Guise's cousin was known.

the rue Bethizy where Coligny lived. They were accompanied by a large escort, and Cosseins had been waiting for their arrival. He knocked on the door and shouted, "Open in the name of the King." A man named Labonne, who was on sentry duty inside the door, opened it and was killed by a stab in his chest. The Duc d'Anjou's Swiss guards rushed in, but when they saw Navarre's Swiss guards they hesitated, and Cosseins ordered his French troops to enter. They did so and shot everybody in sight. The Admiral was in his bedroom already half dressed. His friends had joined him as soon as they heard the disturbance in the street outside the house. Pastor Merlin was praying, and as he heard someone knocking on the front door he said to Coligny, "My Lord it is God who is calling us to his fold." "I have been ready to die for a long time," the Admiral replied, "but all of you my friends must get away as quickly as you can, for there is nothing you can do to help me. I commend my soul to the mercy of God." Nicolas Muss refused to leave him, but the others managed to escape through a skylight in the roof.

Suddenly the door of the bedroom was smashed in and two of the Guises' hired assassins and two others stormed into the room. "Are you the Admiral?" one of them asked Coligny, and when he replied, "Yes, I am," the man hit him on the head with the butt of his gun. Two of the other men lifted the Admiral, who was lying on the floor, stunned but still alive, and threw him out of the window, where he fell at Guise's feet. Having wiped Coligny's face, which had been covered with blood, Guise said, "It's him all right" and kicked him in the face. A few of the crowd who were waiting in the street rushed towards the Admiral's body and mutilated it in every possible way, and a man named Petrucci, a flunky of the Duc de Nevers cut off the head and carried it away to the Louvre, whereupon a crowd of ruffians seized what remained of the Admiral's body, dug knives into it and then dragged it through the streets to the banks of the Seine. The bloodbath had begun in earnest!

Just before dawn someone knocked at the door of the King of Navarre's bedroom in the Louvre, where he and his wife lay awake, having hardly slept all night. Henry opened the door and was confronted by a messenger from King Charles, who said that His Majesty wanted to see him at once. When Henry reached the King's bedroom, Condé was already there, waiting outside the door. Eventually both of them were ushered in, where they found Charles with the Queen Mother and her other son, the Duc d'Anjou, standing behind him.

What then took place has been described by Marguerite de Valois in her *Memoirs*. Charles advanced towards his brother-in-law and Condé dagger in hand, shouting "Mass, death or the Bastille".

Condé was the first to reply. "God will not permit me, my King and My Lord," he said, "to choose the first. The other two choices lie in your discretion which God will wish to moderate by his providence."

Charles raised his right arm as though he was about to stab these two hateful Protestants when Catherine intervened, but not for reasons of mercy. At that moment she would have been just as glad to see her son-in-law stabbed to death as she had been at the murder of Coligny. But this was hardly the right moment. There was no point in killing him at a time when it was not improbable that the Duc de Guise might well become the King of Paris* With some difficulty, for Charles had gone completely berserk, Catherine managed to make him see reason.

While all this was going on the French and Swiss soldiers, almost all of whom had been drinking heavily, ransacked the whole of the Palais du Louvre, killing all the Huguenot noblemen who were staying there as guests of the King and also their servants and retinues. When dawn broke the Louvre was littered with corpses and the streets of Paris running with blood. The murder of Coligny had been the signal for the massacre to begin, and it went on all night. The Catholic 'gentlemen', the soldiers of the royal guard and archers competed with the fury of the people of Paris, who ran through the streets killing every Protestant they could find. According to an entry in the diary of the Spanish Ambassador in Paris. "The blood and death ran through the streets to such an extent that even Their Majesties (referring to Charles and Catherine) were frightened." The plan had succeeded more than they expected. The whole of Paris had gone mad. Nevertheless, from other reliable evidence, the Spanish Ambassador seems to have been mistaken. Neither the King nor his mother gave the

* See *Le massacre de la St Barthelemy* by Phillipe Erlanger.

slightest sign of emotion as they heard outside the Louvre the shots being fired in the streets and the cries of the victims, and Catherine when she saw Coligny's body hanging by its legs from the gallows of Montfaucon showed not the least sign of embarrassment. Sully, who was later to become the head of Henry de Navarre's government after he became the King of France, said that when Catherine de Medici and her ladies-in-waiting walked along some of the streets later that day they noted with lecherous satisfaction 'the manly physique of some of the naked corpses.'

The massacre continued in Paris for several days and spread to some of the provinces, including Lyons, where at least 800 Protestants were killed. The mob marched through the streets headed by priests singing the Te Deum.

There was only one member of the royal family, Henry of Navarre's wife Marguerite, who derived no spontaneous exhilaration from the bloodbath. She had seen her husband, for whom she had no affection whatsoever, taken away as a prisoner, and some of the Protestant noblemen were assassinated under her very eyes, yet, to do her justice, she was genuinely relieved when she learnt that Henry was safe and sound.

A few days later Catherine tried to make her daughter break up the marriage, although it was she, who, for her own political ends, had brought it about. Marguerite, however, would not hear of it and told her mother in no uncertain terms that it was she who had joined them together and that they were not going to be put asunder. Although Marguerite was a foolish and wilful woman, it remains to her credit that she refused to betray her husband in his hour of trial and tribulation, although she did not care for him in the slightest and had never wanted to marry him.

3 Four long years

THE next few days after the Massacre of St Bartholomew had come to an end were not easy ones for Henry of Navarre. Condé decided to abjure the Catholic faith, but Henry, although he agreed to carry out Charles's wishes in every other respect, for the time being refused to concede to the King's command that he too should become a Catholic. Charles was furious and threatened to strangle his brother-in-law unless he gave way, and eventually Henry did so. As he was to say several years later that Paris was worth a mass, no doubt he thought on this occasion that to go on living was equally important, and this is not surprising, for Henry was a master of compromise provided he thought that the cause was a good one and would achieve the end he had in mind. As someone once said of him, if he could not control events he thought it wiser to give in to them. On 29th September, therefore, he went to mass for the first time and, to make matters worse, Catherine was also present, gloating over the discomfiture which he doubtless felt, though he did not betray his feelings in any way whatsoever.

However, that was not all he had to do. The King of France persuaded him, much against his will, to expel all the Protestant pastors from the Béarn and to appoint the Comte de Grammont, a Catholic, Lieutenant-General of his kingdom. His subjects and his followers could not have been blamed had they dishonoured him thereafter, but they were fair-minded enough to realize that he should not be held responsible for such treachery as he was obviously acting under duress. They had known Henry for too long and were so attached to the King whom they had seen grow up as a boy in their province a 'man of the people', that they realized that he was being held

in Paris as a hostage. They were certain that one day he would
come back to his own.

There was one last humiliation still to come. In the spring
of 1573 he was forced to take part in an expedition against La
Rochelle, the bastion of the Protestant rebels. Painful as all this
must have been to him, it does not seem to have affected his
temperament. He remained throughout, as one of his con-
temporaries wrote, 'a cheerful good companion', took everything in his stride and enjoyed making fun of almost everybody.
He spent most of his time hunting or playing tennis. When he
was not doing this he enjoyed many flirtations, particularly
with the lovely Charlotte de Beaune-Semblançay, Baronne de
Sauves.

Nevertheless, life at the Louvre, where he was continually
under the critical eye of Catherine, was anything but pleasant,
and in one of his letters to the Baron de Moissens, with whom he
had spent a few happy years in Coarraze when still a small boy,
he wrote, "The court is the strangest place you could ever see.
Any day one expects to have one's throat cut. It is said that they
are going to kill me."

One thing, however, gave him some hope and encouragement during what was virtually a sentence of four years
imprisonment in the Louvre. He noticed daily the growth of a
more liberal and tolerant attitude towards the Protestants,
which he felt certain would one day save France and enable her
to recover from the parlous state to which the wars of religion
had brought her. Many years were to pass, however, before this
new development bore fruit, and it was Henry himself who by
the Edict of Nantes was to give the Protestants the same civil
rights as those possessed by their Catholic brethren.

In 1573 the throne of Poland became vacant, and the Poles
began to look all over Europe for a new king. The Polish
monarchy was not hereditary, and their sovereigns were
elected by the Diet. When Catherine heard the news she
thought that this was an opportunity not to be lost, and she
seized it with both hands. She decided to put her youngest son,
the Duc d'Anjou, up for election. It was most important from
the point of view of French foreign policy that the throne of
Poland should not pass into the hands of Austria. She therefore
sent Monluc, the Bishop of Valence, to support Anjou's

candidature before the Polish Diet. He arrived, however at a most inauspicious moment. The full details of the massacre of St Bartholomew had only recently reached Poland and feeling was very high there, as the Protestants formed a very sizeable minority and the Polish aristocracy, with the exception of a few bishops, were in favour of religious tolerance.

Nevertheless, partly due to the mistakes made by his opponents and partly to his clever pleading, Monluc was able to win over opinion to his side. He played down the horror of the massacre and absolved Charles IX and his brother from any responsibility for it, saying that the situation in France had been so explosive that stern measures had to be taken. He was also greatly helped by the fact that the other two candidates for the throne were both suspect. Ivan the Terrible who lived up to his name, was the last person in the world the Poles wanted for their king. The other candidate was the Archduke Ernst who was anathema to the Poles merely because he was German, and, as he was also an Austrian prince, he was at once suspect to a country which believed in liberty and freedom. The repressive way in which the Hapsburgs had treated the Bohemians was sufficient warning to any Pole. Anjou's competitors were, therefore, not very formidable and the above considerations were responsible for the Duc, who would not otherwise have had a dog's chance, obtaining a majority and being elected by the Diet.

His reign, however, was but a short one, for on 31st May 1574 Charles IX died. He had been unwell for some time, and the Court had moved from Paris to Vincennes, for Charles was certain that he had not got long to live and the last place in which he wanted to die was the Louvre, where, he said, although no one really believed him, he was perpetually haunted by the memories of that 'criminal night' of 23rd and 24th August 1572. When the news of his brother's death reached Anjou a fortnight later, he decided, against the advice given him by his Polish counsellors, to give up the throne of Poland, whatever the outcome might be; but he kept his decision to himself because he knew that otherwise force might be used to prevent him leaving. On the night of 18th and 19th June, three days after the messenger from Paris had arrived with the news of Charles's death, he slipped out of his Château in

Cracow, accompanied by a few of his closest friends, and galloped all the way to the Austrian frontier.

Before he died Charles sent for his brother-in-law and warned him not to trust his mother-in-law, advice which was superfluous, for Henry knew only too well where he stood vis-à-vis the Queen Mother. Even her favourite son, now become Henry III, referred to Catherine as '*La Serpente*', and had it been possible to think of a more uncomplimentary nickname for her, Henry would certainly have used it. In fact, it was quite impossible to find a better name for her. It described her perfectly.

Navarre must have been waiting for the arrival of the new king of France with considerable interest, if not even with some trepidation, but their first meeting passed off quite smoothly. When at last her son reached Paris, Catherine presented both Henry of Navarre and Condé to him, saying, "I hand these two over to you. I have already warned you about their peculiarities. It is up to you to do what you like with them."

The King, perhaps to their surprise, embraced them both, saying, "I give you both your liberty and I want nothing more from you than that you should like me." Whether or not Henry of Navarre was surprised at the King's reaction is a matter for conjecture, but he was certainly not taken in by it. He knew perfectly well that whatever his brother-in-law's personal feelings might be he was but a pawn in the Queen Mother's hands.

Henry of Navarre may have thought that the court in Charles the IX's reign was 'strange', but it was even more so under the influence of the new King. He himself was effeminate to the extreme, bejewelled and foppish. His court was soon to be known as the most fantastic in Europe. Even his own fortune, which was considerable, and the State treasury were not sufficient to satisfy his love for splendour or the extravagance of his 'little darlings', as his three favourites were usually called. They went from party to party, from fête to fête, from ball to ball and from banquet to banquet. They competed with each other for the most valuable jewellery, the most exquisite perfume and the most elaborate dress. They were even more effeminate than the King himself and were responsible for one of his uncomplimentary nicknames, the 'Prince of Sodom.'

The atmosphere of the court was not one in which Henry of Navarre was likely to feel at home, and to have to live surrounded by these worthless creatures did not make life any more pleasant for him than it had been during the reign of Charles IX. He was a man of the country, his main pursuits were hunting and tennis, and when he was not doing either he spent his time with the ladies and was particularly attracted by Charlotte de Beaune-Semblançay; but even this had its drawbacks. Charlotte who was the daughter of Gabrielle de Sade, an ancestress of the notorious Marquis de Sade, distributed her favours freely, and Navarre had to share them with his other brother-in-law, the Duc d'Alencon, although this was better than nothing for she was only 24 years old and very beautiful.

Shortly after he returned from Poland, Henry III developed a violent hatred for his sister Marguerite and spread all sorts of stories round the court about her amorous escapades, of which he took a great delight in keeping Henry of Navarre well informed. Some of the stories were true, and some were not, but they did not worry her husband. Since the night of the St Bartholomew he had cared less for his wife than he did at the time of his marriage, and that was not much. There was no need to worry, for throughout his whole life he was never to be short of female admirers. Marguerite in her turn consoled herself with a number of lovers, her favourite being Guise. The court was the most perverted and immoral in the whole of Europe, and nothing like it had been seen since the days of the Roman Empire.

The King of Navarre, although he made the best of things while he was there, had already made up his mind by the autumn of 1575 to leave the Court in Paris at the earliest opportunity and go to Nerac, but the escape of the Duc d'Alencon in September had opened the Queen's eyes, and a strict watch was kept on her son-in-law, who was not able to put his plan into effect until the following February.

Two days before 3rd February, which was eventually fixed as 'D Day', Henry made a cunning move in order to allay the suspicions of the King and his mother. During the night he disappeared and took care to ensure that the news was spread round that he had fled. When it reached the King and the

Queen Mother there was pandemonium in the palace. Arrangements had just been made by Catherine – who could not get her
son to take much interest in what was to her a catastrophe – for
a thorough search to be made, when the King of Navarre
walked into the room where they were both arguing about
exactly what should be done when eventually he was caught, as
she was sure he would be. With a broad grin on his face he told
them that he had just found some of the search party and had
brought them back. He was sorry to have caused this unnecessary trouble. He told them that it would have been only
too easy to escape had he wished to do so. On the contrary, he
would always serve them faithfully until he died. Having, he
thought, put the Queen Mother off her guard, he left at dawn
on 3rd February to go stag hunting in the forest of Senlis,
where he hoped to be able to elude his escort and make for the
open country. He managed to get rid of the two equerries,
who on Henri III's instructions were supposed never to leave
him, by sending them to the palace with false messages which
they innocently took without suspecting that something was
brewing. As soon as they had gone, Henry galloped off in the
direction of Poissy accompanied by some of his faithful retinue
(including a young man named Rosny, who was later to become
the famous Duc de Sully and, when Henry became King of
France, his right-hand man, though sometimes also his severest
critic).

At Poissy the party crossed the Seine and continued their
trek in a westerly direction. Many incidents took place on the
way. Near the village of Montfort l'Amoury Henry just missed
being killed by a blow from a bill-hook. On the way to Chateauneuf, when passing through one of the villages, they had an
amusing encounter with an elderly man who happened to be the
local Lord of the Manor whom they had stopped and asked the
way to Chateauneuf. It is probable that the news of Henry's
escape had travelled more quickly than the royal fugitive
himself, for it transpired later that the man in question guessed
that it was the King of Navarre and his party. However, the
company included a Monsieur de Rocquelaure, who was
exceptionally well dressed, and the Lord of the Manor mistook
him for the King.

After he had told them the name of the village the Lord of

the Manor begged the 'King' not to cause any trouble by stopping there, suggested they should carry on until they reached Chateauneuf and offered to show them the way. *En route*, thinking that he was not in earshot of the man whom he had mistaken for the king, he began talking to some of the others, oblivious of the fact that one of them was none other than Henry himself. He talked freely about the stories he had heard of the strange things which went on at the French court and in particular about Marguerite de Valois' many love affairs, causing much amusement in which the King joined. As night was falling they arrived at Chateauneuf, and someone demanded that the gates be opened in the name of the King of Navarre. When their guide, to his astonishment and embarrassment saw Henry enter the town at the head of his men, he realized the gaffe he had made, went down on his knees and begged the King's pardon, which was graciously given. That night the King and his friends had the first decent meal they had been able to get since leaving the Louvre and the Lord of the Manor was asked to join them as a guest. Before he left them next morning, however, he promised faithfully that should any enquiries be made in his village as to whether anyone had seen the King pass through it his lips would be sealed.

On 7th February they arrived in Alençon where they were joined by about 250 of the King's friends and supporters from the districts through which they had passed and even from the court itself. They stayed in Alençon for three days, and fifteen days later reached Saumur, which was the stronghold of the Protestants on the river Loire. Henry decided to make his headquarters there for a few days in order to see how the land lay and make definite plans for the future. When he left Paris it was his intention to take over the government of the Guyenne. This had been given to his father and he had kept it for his son.

While he was in Saumur Henry had a chance to relax for the first time and put behind him the trials and tribulations of the past four years. He could forget the debauchery of the French Court, the machinations of the evil genius behind the throne and the constant fear of assassination. He was even able to escape from the dark shadow of St Bartholomew's Night. As he ironically said to his companions, "I only regret two things: my wife and mass. I need not go to mass any longer; as for my

Henry of Navarre in childhood and youth

The Massacre of St Bartholemew and the murder of Coligny,
seen at left riding his horse, at right being killed and flung
from the window

(*left*) Diane d'Andouins, la Belle Corisande. (*right*) Marguerite
de Valois, Henry's first wife

The Château de Nerac, one of Henry's favourite residences

wife I shall neither be able nor do I want ever to see her again." The only real regret he had was leaving Charlotte de Beaune-Semlançay behind. As for the future, he knew only too well the difficulties ahead but was not dismayed by them.

The first ten years, however, were relatively peaceful in France compared with what was going on in other parts of Europe, where Philip II of Spain was assembling a large fleet in the ports of Portugal and Flanders and gathering a large army for the invasion of England, and in the Low Countries the epic resistance against the Catholic invaders was just beginning. During the whole of this time the King of Navarre had his court at the Château de Nerac in the Guyenne.

But before he reached Nerac and while he was still in Saumur, Catherine had managed, more by force then persuasion, to get her son to come to terms with his Protestant enemies. In a treaty known as 'La Paix de Monsieur'*, signed on 6th May 1576, Henry III disavowed the massacre of St Bartholomew, which, he stated, had been carried out 'much to his annoyance'. By the same treaty, the property of the victims which had then been confiscated was returned to their heirs, and the Protestants were recognized as an important political and administrative minority and were allotted forty-five towns to be regarded as Protestant strongholds spread over six provinces. They were also allowed freedom of worship.

The rebel princes also received recognition, the Duc d'Alençon being given, in addition to the Berry and the Touraine, the Duchy of Anjou; and Condé, who had brought into France an army of *reiters*,† took over the government in Picardy. Damville, the Catholic governor of the Languedoc, was allowed to retain it, and the Guises, who were always in the offing when favours were being distributed, received not less than five of the thirteen provinces of France.

The King of Navarre had ceased to be a practising Catholic, but it was not until the middle of June on his way to Nerac via Niort that he abjured the Catholic faith and returned to the Protestant Church. It was a wise decision, for he had begun to

---

* Its official name was the Treaty of Beaulieu since it had been signed at Beaulieu near Loches. '*Monsieur*' was the name by which the Dauphins of France (the heirs to the throne) were then known.

† German troopers.

be regarded as a suspect by both Catholics and Protestants but especially by the latter, and that he could not afford. In May, d'Aubigné, 'the soldier historian', who had been a member of Henry's escape party, said, "The Court of Saumur had been three months without religion."

It was most important that Henry should win more supporters over to his side, for the battle between Catholics and Protestants was not yet over, and the Protestants would be more likely to follow their former leader but not while he remained a Catholic. Furthermore, he felt that to leave the Catholics could do him little, if any, harm, as they were already his enemies, and he would have no difficulty in winning over the more liberally-minded Catholics to support a policy of greater tolerance towards Protestantism, for so many Frenchmen were getting tired of these religious wars which had brought the economy of France to such a low ebb.

On the way to Nerac from Saumur he took advantage of the visit of his sister, Catherine, to Niort to attend a service in the Protestant church in company with her. From there he made a pilgrimage to La Rochelle, which was the 'holy citadel' of the French Protestants, where he was received, according to Sully, with the same honours which would have been given to the King of France. His views on religion were not those of a fanatical bigot.

> Religion [he once said] is implanted into the hearts of men by the force of doctrine and persuasion and not by the sword. Being all of us Frenchmen we should be able to live in Christian amity. Those who follow their own consciences sincerely are of my religion and I am of the same religion as those who are good and brave.

As usual, the Queen Mother, intent on carrying out her policy of walking the tight rope and alternately trying to please both the Catholics and the Protestants, had, by forcing her son to sign the Treaty of Bealieu, gone too far, and not for the first time. The resentment of the Catholics was soon to make itself felt, and it was not long before Henry III regretted what he had done. He gave practical proof of this by dismissing the Bishop of Limoges who had helped the Queen Mother with the negotiations which led up to this generally unpopular treaty.

The first serious reaction to it took place in Picardy, of which Condé had been made governor, with Peronne as its seat of government. Its inhabitants were not prepared to hand it over to a heretic and formed an organization called The League* to prevent this happening. The main objects of the League, which became very powerful and was later to cause the King of Navarre much trouble after his accession to the French throne in 1589, were to maintain the rights and privileges of the Catholic Church and to ban all the Protestant sects, the members of which it denounced as traitors. Under the leadership of the Duc de Guise and his brother the Cardinal de Lorraine the League became a dangerous threat to the throne. It secretly received subsidies from Spain and was openly encouraged by the Vatican. It conducted a campaign of propaganda against the monarchy, which it accused of being excessively tolerant of heresy, and against the heretics themselves. Starting originally as an organization pledged to defend the Catholic faith it eventually developed into a political party with republican and revolutionary views. It maintained permanent delegates in Rome and Madrid and even went to far as to send secret agents to England to incite the Catholic population to conspire against their Queen. It was not surprising in the circumstances that Henry III, at the instigation of his mother, barely two months after he had been so generous to the Protestants, was now handing over control to those who wished to exterminate them. He had no will of his own and gave way to pressure whenever applied. He was incapable of carrying out a coherent policy.

In 1577 he gave public expression of this by officially acknowledging the League and becoming its head, but it was only a formality. The control still remained in the hands of the two Guises, for the King was incapable of controlling anything.

Meanwhile, the King of Navarre had been concentrating all his energy and talent on the pacification and administration of the Guyenne, which was in a parlous state. Poverty was widespread and political stability non-existent due to the unrest and ravages of the religious wars during which half the province had been laid bare.

It was no easy task, but his moderation and understanding of

* *La Ligue.*

the common people soon enlisted the co-operation of all and sundry – Catholics as well as Protestants, the aristocracy and the peasants – which enabled him in a short time to restore the whole province to a state of order and stability. This co-operation also made it possible for him to make provision for the future by establishing reliable garrisons in places of strategic importance without any opposition except from Bordeaux, whence a protest was sent demanding that the King of Navarre should free the walls of the city. There was, however, one thing which Henry had learnt during his four years exile in the Louvre, namely, patience. He replied to the protest by reminding the civic leaders of the city that it was most important that the whole province should be united and in agreement. "I beg you," he said, "to remember where your duty lies and that from now on the authority of my Lord the King of France should be recognized through me better than it has been in the past." The city's garrison remained.

In all his dealings with the people of the Guyenne he emphasized that there should be a good *entente* between all Frenchmen under the King's authority, although he realized that this might not increase his popularity with the Huguenots. But Henry was not thinking merely of the present, he was looking to the future, the day when he would himself be King of France. Another twelve years were to elapse before he sat on the throne of France, but, unless something unexpected were to happen, it was a practical certainty that one day he would become the heir presumptive to Henry III.

While the King of Navarre was busy consolidating the province of Guyenne, Henry III made many political declarations regarding the necessity to continue having peaceful relations with the Protestants. Secretly, however, he was preparing for war and took steps to establish Catholic Leagues in all the provinces. Many members of the States General*, however, although they were zealous Catholics, were not in favour of pressing too harshly on the Protestants lest it should lead to a new religious war. But eventually they gave in and voted for the subsidies for which the King had asked to keep the army properly equipped and ready for any emergency. Shortly afterwards Henry III came out into the open when, on 29th

* Broadly equivalent to the English parliament.

December 1576, he declared himself against pacification. From this moment until 1584 Catholics and Protestants eyed each other with hatred and distrust, for the King's statement was considered tantamount to a declaration of war.

Henry III's formal disavowal of the '*Paix de Monsieur*' on 16th January 1577 was a great shock to the King of Navarre – even though it may not have entirely surprised him – for it came at a time when he had almost succeeded in making the terms of the peace effective in his province of Guyenne, a task which had not been easy. It had only been accomplished after overcoming resistance and obstruction from both Catholics and Protestants and at the risk of losing popularity in both camps.

The Protestants had been weakened by these divisions, the King of Navarre was not in a position to end them, and fighting had broken out again. Even in La Rochelle, the stronghold of the reformation in France, the Protestants were divided. The rich bourgeoisie were in favour of peace, the people wanted war, but they called for warlike action without being prepared for it. The inhabitants of La Rochelle refused to receive the Prince de Condés troops, and not without reason, for they had recently ravaged the surrounding country. The fighters on both sides thought only of plunder and pillaged both friends and enemies.

Except in the Languedoc the Catholics had several successes between April and August, and La Rochelle capitulated after severe fighting on August 24th. However, the Protestants in the Languedoc and the Cevennes, commanded by a son of Admiral de Coligny, resisted with more success, but by September, their position having become hopeless, they surrendered, and a peace treaty was signed at Bergerac on 17th September 1577.

The Edict of Poitiers, which ratified the treaty, took away many of the freedoms which the Protestants had obtained by the Treaty of Beaulieu. They no longer had unrestricted freedom of worship, but they were still allowed to retain for another six years their eight Protestant strongholds. Henry III was delighted with the outcome of the war and called the Treaty of Bergerac 'My Peace'. Nevertheless, the Catholics had gained nothing by their victory, for by article 56 of the Edict of Poitiers the Leagues were abolished.

As a result of this treaty many of the provinces lost some of
their independence, and the King of Navarre complained that
he was the governor of the Guyenne in name only. Bordeaux
refused to receive him, and Maréchal Biron, his Lieutenant-
General, continued to take orders direct from Paris.

In the Languedoc guerilla fighting continued in spite of the
treaty; Coligny's son refused to disarm; the Protestants, who
were better trained than the Catholics, terrorized the province;
and marauding bands ravaged the countryside. According to
a report laid before the States General by the deputies of the
Languedoc, the ground was covered with the blood of poor
peasants, women and little children. Towns and villages were
left in ruins, most of the houses having been destroyed by fire,
and all this had happened since the signing of the treaty.

These acts were committeed [the report continued] not by
Tartars, Turks and Muscovites but by persons born and brought
up in this country who profess to practice what is called the
'reformation religion' which by the monstrous and wicked manner
of living of its members has become infamous and odious in the
eyes of God and the whole world.

4 Private lives

SHORTLY after the signing of the treaty the King of Navarre returned to his little Court at Nerac, where he hoped, at last, to have some rest and quiet, to 'live like a gentleman' without any ceremony and to give himself a good time, as he wrote in a letter to one of his friends. For the next seven years his hopes were realized. For a man of his tastes and pursuits there could have been no better place to indulge in them than at the Château de Nerac, built by his ancestors, standing in the most beautiful grounds and surrounded by large woodlands full of game of every description.

He lived the life of a country gentleman, hunting and playing his favourite game of tennis, and visiting the '*bons seigneurs*' in the neighbourhood. He accepted every invitation and received many in return for his presence at a party made certain of its success, and he was just as much at home when he attended a village fête as he was at a ball given by one of the *bourgeoisie* in Agen. But his greatest passion was a day's hunting which was generally followed by a gargantuan repast, some of the menus of which still exist. On one of these occasions Henry and his guests sat down at table faced with 180 pounds of beef, 74 of veal, 295 of mutton, 13 kids, 9 turkeys, 200 capons, 11 rabbits, 10 quails, 18 partridges and 24 teals. How many litres of wine they washed it all down with was not recorded.

Nevertheless, life was not all fun and games. His entourage at the château included both Catholics and Protestants, and, although for a time they appeared to enjoy peaceful coexistence, it was, as the word itself suggests, liable to break down at any time. It was not long before rifts began to appear, and many unfortunate incidents occurred. Nor was this all. Although Henry's pleasant manners, gaiety and good humour were appreciated by many people and were responsible for his popularity, there were others who disliked these qualities. Bordeaux, the capital of the province, once again shut its gates against him.

The French court then began to be a nuisance. They were not happy at the apparent success of the young governor's policies, so they decided to appoint Biron Lieutenant-General of the province and sent him to Nerac to keep a strict eye on Henry. Catherine was also annoyed with her son-in-law because of his indifference towards Marguerite, his wife, whom he appeared to have forgotten since leaving Paris, and she decided to go to Nerac and find out exactly what was going on. Hoping that a reconciliation between the royal couple, even if it were purely formal, might help the cause of peace, she took her daughter with her.

Their first meeting took place at La Réole on 2nd October 1578, and it passed off with only one unpleasant incident. The King of Navarre was quite cordial and seemed pleased to see his wife and mother-in-law, who congratulated him for the part he had played in carrying out the provisions of the Edict of Poitiers in the province of Guyenne. However, when Biron, who, unknown to the King, had accompanied Catherine on the journey from Paris, suddenly appeared, the King's manner completely changed, and Marguerite had the greatest difficulty in keeping the peace.

From La Réole they proceeded to Auch, where, at a ball given by Madame la Barthe, Henry fell madly in love with a Cypriot, Dayolle, who was one of the Queen Mother's ladies-in-waiting. The return of Marguerite to her husband had obviously not had any effect, and there was a further complication, for the lady-in-waiting who had accompanied Catherine was none other than Charlotte de Sauves, also one of Henry's part-time women. The Queen Mother knew only too well that an affair had been going on between these two for several months before her son-in-law left Paris, so she must have brought Charlotte with her for a definite purpose. What it was can only be a matter of conjecture, but it is not beyond the bounds of possibility that it was to get her away, at least for a time, from the Duc d'Alençon, with whom Henry of Navarre had had to share Charlotte's favours at the Louvre. Catherine

was not worried about what Marguerite might think. Her
marriage to Henry was purely a political one, and the Queen
Mother knew that her daughter never found any difficulty
in having a man about the house. For Henry himself it could
not have been better, for this time the boot was on the other
leg. He no longer had to share Charlotte with Alençon, she now
had to share him with Dayolle.

Catherine's decision to go to Nerac was not, however, made
solely with the object of trying to bring about a reconciliation
between Marguerite and Henry. She had every intention of
combining business with pleasure, and find out for herself the
influence of the Huguenots in the south of France. She would
then be able to decide whether it was better to create discord
and suspicion between the rival leaders of the Protestants,
Condé and the King of Navarre, or keep them quiet by
granting concessions. That was the real reason for her journey,
and the reinstatement of her daughter in her rightful place as
Queen of Navarre was merely the cover plan.

Marguerite herself did not want to leave Paris and spend the
rest of her life in the stuffy atmosphere of a provincial court.
She soon found out that her husband, during the last two and a
half years, had not missed her any more than she had missed
him and had enjoyed being a grass-widower. It was obvious,
as she wrote in her *Memoirs*, that he paid far more attention to
the attractive bevy of beautiful girls whom her mother had
brought with her than he did to his wife.

Catherine, however, was far too busy to notice this. She was
concentrating on attaining her first objective, which was to try
and bring about a reconciliation between the King of Navarre
and the newly-appointed Lieutenant-General of the province,
Maréchal de Biron. This she found quite impossible. The Queen
Mother had now been at Nerac for more than two months, and
time was running short as she had other places to visit before
returning to Paris to look after her son Henry III, who needed
to be kept under close supervision. She therefore lost no time
in getting down to brass tacks and started negotiations with the
Catholics and Protestants of Guyenne and Languedoc. The
delegates from the Languedoc churches presented a long list of
their complaints, but the King of France's advisers – amongst
whom was the Cardinal de Bourbon, who was accompanying

Catherine on her tour of the south – rejected most of these demands by relying on the provisions of the Edict of Poitiers.

The Queen Mother took a leading part in the negotiations, alternately threatening and appeasing both sides, so that eventually, with the assistance of the King of Navarre, who was convinced that a policy of moderation was the right one to adopt in the circumstances, the Protestants were induced to cut down their demands. Nevertheless, above all else they wanted two things, freedom of worship throughout the whole kingdom and control of more towns than they had been given under the provisions of the Edict of Poitiers. Catherine refused to grant them freedom of worship, but she agreed to let them have control of fifteen more towns though only for six months. The Protestant delegates agreed to these conditions, and a treaty embodying them was signed at Nerac on 21st February 1579.

Catherine left Nerac apparently satisfied with the result of her stay there, but she must have realized, for she was no fool, that the Protestants had only agreed to her conditions, with Henry's approval, from expediency, and that it was most improbable that they would surrender the fifteen strongholds after the six months had elapsed.

After his mother-in-law had gone Henry was able to go back to the normal life of a country gentleman, but in very different surroundings. The château was completely refurnished to satisfy Marguerite's luxurious taste. Large tapestries and Venetian mirrors with gold frames hung on the walls of all the rooms, and the tables were littered with classical books. An army of cooks invaded the kitchens, and the vineyards of Gascony and Guyenne were stripped to fill the wine cellars. But there was no longer the homely atmosphere that Henry enjoyed more than anything else. Pomp and ceremony were the order of the day, and he hated them both. The royal couple lived their own lives and had their own lovers and mistresses, and there was no secret about it.

It was during a short visit to Pau, however, shortly after Catherine's departure, that their first quarrel occurred, and it must have reminded Henry of the differences which his father and mother frequently had, for it was about religion. They stayed in Pau for less than three weeks, but that was quite long enough for Marguerite. Somehow or other the ghost of Jeanne

d'Albret seemed to haunt the château, and the mere mention of
the word Catholic was almost regarded as blasphemous. They
were in Pau during Whitsun, and with great difficulty the
Queen managed to arrange for mass to be said in the Chapel so
that she could take communion. As she left after the service the
gentlemen of her suite, who had attended mass with her, were
arrested and put in prison. When asked by his wife to have them
released Henry reluctantly agreed to have this done, but not
before he had told her in no uncertain terms what he thought
about her and the Catholics.

Peaceful co-existence between Catholic and Protestant
obviously did not, like charity, begin at home.

On the return of Henry and Queen Margot* to Nerac,
however, she was able to console herself with the pleasures of
the court, which, as she wrote in her *Memoirs* "so much re-
sembled the French Court" that she no longer felt miserable
away from the Louvre. She even managed to change her
husband's way of living to some extent. He still hunted and
played tennis, but his manners, dress, and general behaviour
completely altered. Previously he had worn nothing but simple
country clothes. The large wardrobes in his bedchamber were
now full of black and white satin doublets, linen shirts from
Holland, yellow satin breeches, silk stockings, velvet hats
decked with feathers and scarlet cloaks with gold and silver
embroidery. He even abandoned his rough country manners,
moderated his language and could be seen bowing and scraping
like all the other bedecked, perfumed and overdressed courtiers
whom Margot had brought with her from Paris. He hated it all
but did it to please his wife. She even tried to get her husband to
use scent because, she said, when she kissed him when he returned from the hunt, covered with dust and dripping with
sweat, it made her feel quite sick. This, however, he flatly
refused to do.

Having gone to such lengths to please her, he saw no reason
why he should be faithful to her, and he continued to have
numerous affairs. When the Queen Mother left Narac she
took Charlotte de Sauves with her, which did not worry Henry
very much as she had ceased to have any attraction for him,

* This was the name by which she was generally known when she came
to Nerac.

and Catherine had left a substitute behind. This was the Cypriot, Victoria d'Ayola Dayolle to whom Henry had taken an immediate fancy when they met at La Réole. But she was by no means the only one who received the King's favours. There were four others, Jeanne de Monceau, Catherine du Lac, Anne de Balsac de Montaigu and Armandine d'Agen. However, none of them had managed to win the way to his heart, and he had recently been attracted by the charm of Mademoiselle de Rebours, about whom Margot said spitefully but also with some justification, "This malicious girl who had an intense dislike for me did all she could to demean me in the eyes of my husband."

During Madamoiselle de Rebour's short reign as Henry's favourite mistress Margot consoled herself with the young Vicomte de Turenne, a distant cousin, who had been a childhood friend of hers at the Louvre. During the next three years of mutual indifference and tolerance, prior to Marguerite leaving Nerac and returning to Paris, there were occasions on which she was a good wife to him, despite all she had suffered. When her husband was taken ill with a high fever when he visited Eauze, she left Nerac as soon as she heard of his illness and never left his bedside until he recovered seventeen days later. This was more than generous of her. Little did she know that within a few weeks a new affair with a young girl named Fosseuse was about to begin.

Her real name was Francoise de Montmorency-Fosseuse, and she was one of Marguerite's maids of honour. She was only fifteen years old when the King first took a fancy to her, but for a time it was an innocent fancy. It took him a long time to recover from his illness, and during his convalescence she used to come and visit him in his bedroom and sit on his knee. He called her his 'little girl'. Marguerite encouraged this as long as it continued in that way, but as Henry gradually got better he saw 'La Fosseuse' in a different light, and in December 1581 she bore him a child. Marguerite, who by then was getting very tired of Nerac, thought the opportunity was too good to miss and made this an excuse for leaving her husband. In March 1582 she returned to Paris via Fontainebleau.

Meanwhile feelings between Catholics and Protestants had been running high since 1578 and a further outbreak of war did not seem distant. The moment had arrived when the Huguenots had only two choices left to them, either to hand back the towns which had been temporarily conceded to them by the Edict of Poitiers or to hold them by force of arms. Hence the war, which became known as '*La Guerre des Amoureux*'* and began on 28th May 1580 with the siege of Cahors. It got its name for the following reason. Henry III's chief amusement was to tell stories about the court at Nerac and its 'indiscretions', which exasperated his sister Marguerite, La Fosseuse, who heard of the scandals through the Queen, had passed them on to Navarre and to all the ladies of the Court, who, it is said, used all their influence, which was not inconsiderable to provoke a rupture.†

The King of Navarre himself and his advisers realized that they had either to honour the provisions of the Edict of Nerac, which Catherine de Medici had negotiated in 1579, or take the offensive. They decided in favour of war. On 28th May 1580 the King of Navarre suddenly appeared before the gates of Cahors with an army of several thousand men. The town, which was well situated on the banks of the river Lot, was defended by a strong garrison commanded by an experienced soldier, Jean de Vezins. The Huguenot forces blew down the gates with petards,‡ and the battle continued in the streets and on the barricades for four days and nights. The inhabitants of Cahors, who had been issued with arms, joined in the fighting, put up a heroic resistance, and the result of the battle was uncertain for some time, but early on the morning of the fifth day of siege the garrison surrendered. So severe was the fighting that the attacking army suffered more severe casualties than the defending garrison. Henry of Navarre, as well as commanding the Protestant army, took a personal part in the fighting, as one would have expected him to do, and the encouragement which this gave his troops was largely responsible for their victory. It also marked a decisive stage in his career; he came out of the battle with the reputation of a fine soldier and a competent commander and convinced the Béarnais that there was good reason for them to have confidence henceforth in their leader.

* The Lovers' War.
† *Histoire de France* by Ernest Lavisse, Vol. VI, p. 198.
‡ A former engine of war used to blow down doors, etc.

The taking of Cahors was not important in itself, but it left no doubt in Henry III's mind that from now on they had someone to reckon with.

Apart from this one victory, 'The Lover's War' was disastrous for the Protestants for they came out of it with their influence greatly diminished, and the Treaty of Fleix, which was signed in November 1580, gave them nothing new. All it did was to confirm the Treaty of Nerac and leave them in control of their strongholds for another six months.

After Henry of Navarre had signed the treaty he returned to the Château de Nerac. He began to prepare for the next move and no longer had to put up with the constant opposition from his former Lieutenant-General, Biron, as he had been recalled to Paris, and a new one, Matignon, had been sent to relieve him. Fortunately for Navarre, Matignon gave him full co-operation, and this made things much easier.

It was shortly after this that La Fosseuse began to show signs of being with child. Marguerite told her mother all about it and suggested that she should come back to the Louvre at least for a short time. The Queen Mother agreed, but as usual there was an ulterior motive behind her decision. She hoped that if Marguerite returned to Paris it might later lead to her son-in-law coming to join his wife, and this was something she wanted more than anything else. Henry of Navarre had now become someone to be reckoned with, and to have had him at the Louvre more or less under her thumb would have been most useful in the event of her wishing to have another confrontation with the Protestants or to face up to the Guises, whose growing influence was becoming a menace to the Crown. Perhaps she might succeed where Henry III had failed, for he had already tried to get his brother-in-law to return to the French court without any success.

When, therefore, Catherine wrote and invited her daughter to return, she sent 15,000 écus to cover the expenses of the journey and expressed the hope that the King of Navarre would consider leaving his province for a few weeks and accompany his wife as far as Saint Maixent in the Poitou, where the Queen Mother would come and meet them both. With typical cunning '*La Serpente*' insisted that Marguerite should bring La Fosseuse with her, thinking that this would make it almost

certain that her son-in-law would make the journey – and she
was right. Henry, frightened that he might lose his mistress,
agreed with the Queen Mother's suggestion and left the
Château de Nerac with a large retinue, including Mademoiselle
de Montmorency. During the journey Marguerite put on a mask
of graciousness, and the party arrived at Saint Maixent without
incident and apparently in harmony to await Catherine's
arrival. A fortnight elapsed before she got there, during
which time a good slice of the 15,000 écus was spent on having
a good time and inviting all the local gentry to dinners and
receptions. On 28th March 1582 the Queen Mother reached
Saint Maixent but only stayed for three nights and left for
Fontainebleau without accomplishing her mission, for Henry
steadfastly refused to accompany his wife and mother-in-law to
Paris. Catherine achieved one thing, however, as he had to say
goodbye to La Fosseuse, who, for some reason or other, decided to remain with the Queen of Navarre.

When Henry said goodbye to his mistress he burst into tears,
but once he was back in Nerac he soon forgot her and resumed
the life of a bachelor, which undoubtedly suited his nature and
his temperament better than being a husband. He hunted,
played tennis and had various affairs with the ladies of his
Court without, however, forming any special attachment to any
of them until, in the summer of 1583, he fell in love with Diane
d'Andoins, the widow of Philibert de Grammont, Comte de
Guiche, who had been killed three years before during the
siege of La Fère. Diane, who was always known as Corisande,
was to take a unique place in his life, for, although she was only
his mistress, she became more than a wife to him and for seven
years was his 'guide, philosopher and friend.' "If I say she was
a friend," Montaigne wrote, "I do so by design, for she was not
merely his mistress in the accepted sense of the word. . . . What
she liked about him was his bravery and character rather than
his caresses." She truly loved Henry for himself, was devoted to
him and, being an extremely intelligent woman, was always
at hand to give him sound advice, which he never disregarded
without giving it careful consideration.

The next twelve months were busy ones for Henry, who had
begun to realize that his image in other European Countries
was not of the best due to the constant propaganda which

Condé had been studiously disseminating about the court at
Nerac. In order to counter such propaganda, Henry sent his
own ambassadors to England, Switzerland, Germany, Denmark and Sweden. Their task was to give a true picture of
Navarre and its king, and to inform those countries of his plans
for the future.

Nor was this all. The time was drawing nigh when the
Huguenots would have to surrender the places which under
various edicts they had been allowed to keep for six years.
Henry of Navarre had no intention of surrendering them, for
to do so would have weakened the position of the Protestants
in the south-west of France. He had to decide whether it would
be wiser to 'wait and see' or to take the initiative, remembering
the well-known military maxim that 'offensive is the best
method of defence'. To await developments would, probably,
have been the better course to have adopted had he been able
to depend on Matignon's co-operation, but he could no longer
count on it. For some time ago his new Lieutenant-General
had changed his attitude, and he had become as difficult as
Biron had been. This was doubtless due to instructions which
he had received from the Queen Mother, who was up to her
old tricks again.

To deal with this difficult situation he decided to do two
things. He told his Protestant delegates in Paris – who were
carrying out negotiations there with the Catholics – that they
should give the impression that they were in a conciliatory
mood yet, at the same time, leave it in no doubt that they were
not prepared to make any concessions without a '*quid pro quo*'.
At the same time he stiffened his policy within the province of
Guyenne and began a series of military operations, knowing
full well that any opposition to them by Henry III would be
half-hearted because the King did not want a certain family
scandal to come out into the open as it was he himself who
had so imprudently started it.

This he had done one evening during a ball given at the
Louvre, when he openly reproached his sister for the immoral
life she was leading and disclosed the names of her lovers. He
then told her to leave as she was no longer wanted. As soon as
she had gone, the King wrote to his brother-in-law and told
him that his wife had left, without mentioning the provocation

which had caused her decision. He received a polite reply from Henry de Navarre, who wrote a letter of thanks saying that he was very pleased to hear that Marguerite was returning to him. "I want her here very much" he wrote, "and she cannot come too soon."

Very shortly afterwards the news of the scandal reached Nerac, and it was not long before Henry de Navarre heard about it and immediately wrote to the King asking for more details. The King's reply was more offensive than the original imputations. Although he tried to excuse himself by stating that the scandal was the work of notorious gossip-mongers at the French court which had not convinced him, it was not only Marguerite who was involved but the former Queen of Navarre, Henry of Navarre's mother, Jeanne d'Albret.

The King of Navarre was furious. "A hotch-potch of non-sense" he called it, and he wrote a letter to the King in no uncertain terms. "His Majesty has honoured me by writing all these letters first of all informing me that I am a cuckold and then that I am the son of a whore, for which I thank him."

A few days later, on 20th November 1583, Henry of Navarre captured the town of Mont de Marsan, which had been con-ceded to the Huguenots by the Treaty of Fleix, but which, in fact, had never been handed over to them. This was im-mediately countered by Matignon, who stationed Catholic troops in Bazas. The King of Navarre ordered their immediate withdrawal and threatened to call off the negotiations still taking place in Paris unless Bazas was immediately handed back, but Henry III took no notice and ordered the occupation of two other towns, including Agen – which was most important because of its proximity to Nerac – then himself ended the Protestant-Catholic conference and sent his brother-in-law's delegation back to the Guyenne.

The stiffening attitude on the King's part, as on so many other occasions, was not maintained for long, and he had, in all probability, only adopted it out of spleen. He had no sound judgment and generally acted purely on impulse. He had been made a fool of, not for the first time, by his brother-in-law, for whom, strangely enough, he still had a sneaking regard, and he had been hurt and embarrassed by Navarre's stern reaction to his scarcely concealed imputations against Jeanne d'Albret,

E

whose faults, whatever they had been, were not of the flesh. Before two months had elapsed there was a temporary reconciliation between them. Henry III restarted the negotiations which he had called off, while the King of Navarre accepted the explanation which his brother-in-law gave – although he did not for a moment believe it – that his accusations against Marguerite and her mother-in-law had been due to an unfortunate misunderstanding. Navarre's generosity paid a handsome dividend, for the royalist troops were withdrawn from all the Protestant towns which they had occupied and Marguerite returned to Nerac.

The evidence regarding her husband's innermost thoughts when Marguerite arrived, which can only be a matter for conjecture, is too contradictory for any conclusion to be drawn from it. She was, however, in tears. Were they tears of sorrow or of joy? It is not unlikely that they were both. As far as Henry was concerned, she would probably be less of a danger at the Court of Navarre than at the Louvre. For her any change was better than none.

5 The heir presumptive

On 10th June 1584, François de Valois, Duc d'Anjou, Catherine de Medici's youngest son and Henry III's sole surviving brother died. Since Henry had no children after six years of a sterile marriage, and there was little likelihood that he would, the next heir to the throne would almost certainly be Henry of Navarre. The view of the League was that it would be better if France were to become a republic rather than that it should be governed by a Huguenot king.

The King had come to the conclusion that he would rather his brother-in-law succeeded him than the Duc de Guise and tried to find ways and means of getting his successor on his side. According to the Salic Law* Henry of Navarre was the heir presumptive. The only practical obstacle to his succession was the fact that he was a heretic, and the King sent his favourite friend and counsellor, d'Epernon, to Nerac to try and get his brother-in-law, once again, to abjure the Protestant faith and become a Catholic. The King of Navarre gave an audience to d'Epernon, but refused to become a Catholic. This decision was, doubtless, influenced by an important consideration, apart from any question of conscience. To become a Catholic would certainly alienate his Protestant subjects without gaining him the support of the Catholics. In any event – and this was probably the most important factor when making his decision, for he was, above all else, a realist – the time was not yet ripe.

When d'Epernon returned to Paris with the news Henry III refused publicly to acknowledge the King of Navarre as his successor but remained friendly with him and even agreed to a

* The Salic Law laid it down that the throne of France could not be occupied by a woman.

reunion of an *Assemblée Generale* to be held at Montauban.

After the death of his brother, Henry III's position on the throne of France was most precarious. He was now thirty-three years old, and his reputation, not only throughout his own kingdom but outside its frontiers, was an object of scandal. Was he man, was he woman, or was he both in one, everybody wondered. In all the contemporary court paintings he is portrayed surrounded by his effeminate 'little darlings'. He was cruel and treacherous, yet sometimes he could be kind and generous. He adored birds and other animals, and the Louvre was full of them. Many, but not all, of his weaknesses were due to his mother, who spoilt him as a child and still, when he was King, idolized him. He was attached to her by a 'silver cord'. Many people suspected that he was a homosexual, but there is no evidence to support this, and there is another explanation of his predilection for being surrounded by effeminate young men. He was terrified of women, though he was happy with his wife, the virtuous Louise de Vaudemont, a princess of the House of Lorraine and the sister of Henry of Guise. In 1582 he had travelled on foot all the way from Paris to Chartres in the depths of winter to pray Notre Dame de Sous-Terre for a virility which he was convinced only a miracle could give him.

Disappointed with the King's weakness and vacillation, the Catholic League turned against him and tried to divide the royal family by approaching the Queen Mother and asking her to stop her son making more concessions to the Protestants. It was perhaps because he realized his unpopularity that during this period he treated his brother-in-law with respect and even made him a present of 100,000 écus, although it must have been a heavy strain on his resources, which were at that time very meagre. He also extended by two years the date which had been fixed by the Treaty of Fleix for handing over control of some of the Protestant strongholds. He did all this with no enthusiasm, however, but merely because he hoped it might secure him a valuable and much-needed ally. His enemies, and particularly the Guises, were saying that when he had sent d'Epernon to see the king of Navarre it was with the object of confirming him in his heresy rather than converting him to the 'true faith'. They feared that Navarre's accession to the throne would see the end of Roman Catholicism, but in this they were proved wrong.

Almost immediately after he had succeeded Pope Gregory XIII, the new Pontiff, Sixtus V, prevailed upon by the Catholic League, issued a papal bull excommunicating Henri de Bourbon* and the Prince de Condé and declaring the former incapable of sitting on the throne of France. Many of the Pope's cardinals were strongly against such precipitate action and thought it would better to wait the turn of events. The Pope had gone too far and had no idea what a storm he had started.

He was attacked from almost every quarter. The celebrated Huguenot jurist, Hotman, wrote a pamphlet protesting against what he called "the stupid thunderbolt of Pope Sixtus V". A Gallican† named Pierre de l'Estoile, who in his *Memoirs* later wrote a daily chronicle of Paris and the French court under Henry III and Henry IV, also attacked His Holiness. It was in the form of a proclamation which he managed to have posted up all over Rome, including the Vatican itself. "Henry IV", the poster proclaimed, "maintains that by accusing him of heresy, Monsieur Sixte, the so-called Pope, had maliciously and atrociously lied. It was he who was the heretic."

The Gallicans were horrified to see the reappearance of the doctrines of theocracy and pontifical omnipotence.

Even the French Parliament found occasion to protest at one and the same time against the "weakness of the King and the audacity of the Pope."

Meanwhile things had not been going too well for Marguerite, who, ever since her return to Nerac in March 1585, had been fighting an incessant war against both her brother and her husband. Life became so difficult, and she resented the close relationship between her husband and Corisande so much that she left Nerac and went to Agen, which she tried to seize on behalf of The League. This attempt was completely unsuccessful. She finally retired to the Château d'Usson, in the Auvergne, and it was not until twenty years later that she again became involved in the life of her husband.

* In the Papal Bull Henry was not referred to as King of Navarre.

† The Gallicans were a sect in the French Roman Catholic Church who were against Papal supremacy.

In 1586 the Queen Mother decided to pay another visit to her son-in-law and arranged to meet him at the Château de Saint-Brice near Cognac, where she arrived with a large retinue of maids of honour. He arrived unescorted and greeted his mother-in-law with great deference but was prepared to deal firmly with her should it become necessary. Catherine kissed him affectionately and asked him to sit down by her surrounded by all the ladies. After a few awkward questions which Navarre adroitly avoided answering, Catherine at last came to the point. She assured him that both she and the King held him in the highest regard and she intended to end the intermittent war which had been going on between Catholics and Protestants for the last eighteen months. She undertook to order the Duc de Joyeuse to withdraw his army from the Poitou – where he had been sent to deal with the King of Navarre's supporters – provided he would return to the court at the Louvre as the acknowledged heir presumptive and stop all military operations in the Guyenne and the Béarn. The right of the Protestants to worship freely in these provinces would, of course, again be withdrawn. She must have known what the result of this meeting with Navarre would be, but Catherine never knew when she was beaten and even when she was she never admitted defeat.

The Queen Mother then dismissed Navarre to give him time to think it all over, but another meeting took place next day when Condé was also present. From the moment of Catherine's arrival at the Château de Saint-Brice the King of Navarre had posted his cousin and 400 soldiers on the neighbouring slopes from which they had a commanding view of the château. Catherine cannot have been unaware of this, for they could be seen from the windows of the drawing room where the meeting was taking place.

When Catherine reopened the conference Navarre and Condé both told her that they were not prepared to make any promises until after the Reformed Churches Assembly had met – which would not be for another two months — but Henry's mind was already made up. He had never forgotten the massacre of St Bartholomew and the humiliation to which he had been subjected while he was kept as a hostage in the Louvre from 1572 until 1576, and he said to the Queen

Mother, "Madame, the only thing for which you can reproach me is that I once trusted you. I do not complain about your credibility but of your age and what it has done to your memory. You have the gift of forgetting your promises and undertakings."

And so they parted, Henry to take counsel with his advisers while Catherine hurried back to Paris to try and persuade her son to make new concessions to the King of Navarre, who, she knew within her heart of hearts, did not trust her half way round the corner – and the fighting, which had temporarily been suspended during the conference, was resumed.

The League had raised three new armies against Navarre and the Protestants. One was made responsible for the defence of Paris and particularly the King of France himself; another was sent to th: Guyenne to deal with Navarre's own army, while the third, under the command of Henri de Guise, was despatched to defend France's eastern frontiers against bands of mercenaries which the other Protestant princes had promised to send to reinforce their French co-religionists.

Henry III, however, could not find the necessary funds to equip and supply these new armies and keep them on a war footing. He was willing, he said, to support them "with his last shirt," but that did not amount to much. He tried to get The League to raise the money, but it did not seem very keen to do so. Its members were even more anxious than he was to carry on fighting the Huguenots but objected to being asked to pay the cost of the campaign.

Immediately after the Queen Mother's departure, Henry of Navarre left the province of Guyenne and set up his head-quarters in the Saintonge, from where he directed operations during the following two months. This resulted in the taking of twenty towns there and in the Poitou. While these operations were going on he wrote a letter to his friend and supporter, the Duc de Montpensier, giving him a brief account of the campaign, and said that he had not slept in his bed during the last two weeks. In addition to these successes, Turenne, who strangely enough had previously been one of Marguerite's lovers – thus illustrating the proverb that "All's fair in love and war" – had recaptured several other towns in Gascony, including Castillon, which, according to one contemporary historian, cost Mayenne* more than 200,000 écus, while all Turenne had to spend was 4 écus, the price of a scaling ladder.

Meanwhile Henry III had established himself on the river Loire with a large force with the object of preventing the Huguenots joining up with the Germans, who were supposed to be coming to reinforce their fellow Protestants. The King, who wanted the best of both worlds, expected that the Duc de Joyeuse would be able to contain Navarre in Poitou, and secretly hoped that Henry de Guise would be defeated by the invading German army, but not before he had inflicted serious casualties on it. He would then intervene at the most opportune moment and lay down the law to both sides. However, Joyeuse, who was an ardent Catholic, disregarded his King's orders to remain on the defensive, and this proved his undoing. Meanwhile the King of Navarre had been reinforced by some troops raised by his cousin the Comte de Soissons. Soissons was, in fact, himself a Catholic, but he was not happy about the Guises' ambition to become the royal family of France, and he had refused to support The League. Nevertheless, even with these reinforcements Navarre's army was no larger than that of his opponent.

Joyeuse, knowing that Navarre had left La Rochelle and was marching towards the Guyenne, set off in pursuit in the hope of cutting off the Huguenot's route to the south. The King of Navarre's intention was to march southwards through the Guyenne and the Languedoc, thus hoping to avoid Joyeuse, and then swing northwards to join up with the Germans. He was following the same plan which Coligny had adopted in the campaign of 1569. Joyeuse's advance guard came upon a patrol of the Huguenot army at Coutras and decided to attack without taking stock of the situation, and without waiting, as he had been ordered to do, for Matignon to reinforce him. Had he only done what he was told the result of the battle of Coutras might well have been different. Matignon was still governing the Guyenne and had a large force at his disposal, and had Joyeuse only been a little less impatient the King of Navarre

---

* The Duc de Mayenne (brother of Henri de Guise) a prominent Leaguer who later, on the accession of the King of Navarre to the throne of France, proclaimed the Cardinal of Bourbon king under the name of Charles X.

would probably have found himself surrounded on both flanks. However, Joyeuse thought that his army of 10,000 men was strong enough to deal with the Huguenots without the help of Matignon. He had gained touch with the Huguenot army on 11th October 1587 and decided to attack on the morrow.

Navarre fully appreciated the situation and realized that Matignon could not be far off, but he was determined to stand and fight. It was a question of 'do or die'. Nevertheless, when he ordered his troops to take up positions to meet the attack on the following morning the King of Navarre knew that he had certain tactical advantages. His artillery had taken up its positions on a hill facing the village of Coutras which completely dominated the plain below it. His left flank was protected by the river Isle and his right flank by thick scrub. Between these two positions he had stationed most of his infantry just over the crest of the hill behind his artillery, where they were hidden from view, and he held three squadrons of cavalry in reserve.

On the morning of the battle he addressed his troops.

"Comrades," he said, "we are here for the glory of God and our honour. The road is open before you. On you go in the name of the Lord for whom we are fighting."

Shortly after dawn Joyeuse launched his attack and began to advance up the hill towards the Huguenot artillery, while Henry and his infantry waited for them and, when they were within range, opened fire on them. They had already suffered heavy casualties from the artillery fire. As they tried to advance towards the crest of the hill they were decimated by the fire of the Huguenots' arquebuses,* whereupon the Huguenot cavalry charged. Within two hours, after a *mêlée* of hand-to-hand fighting, all was over and the Catholic army was completely routed. Nearly all its commanders, including the Commander-in-Chief, Joyeuse, were killed. The Huguenots only admitted having suffered some twenty-five fatal casualties.

The battle of Coutras was the first time Henry of Navarre had been able to show his mettle as a fine soldier and a capable commander. He had behaved, one of his staff said, "like a great captain". Not only had he directed the whole operation, he had also won the admiration of all his troops by his personal

* An early type of portable gun supported on a tripod or a forked rest: *The Concise Oxford Dictionary*.

bravery in the face of the enemy, "fighting like a simple soldier" as one of them said. The Catholics left behind them on the field of battle 2,000 dead and masses of arms and equipment.

The King of Navarre was magnanimous in victory. He praised the courage of the defeated army and set free without ransom those who had been taken prisoner. This was the attitude he adopted throughout the whole of his military career – never to humiliate a defeated enemy. Later that day when he stood before the body of Joyeuse, which was laid out in a room of the Château de Coutras, he said to some of his *seigneurs* who were standing by laughing and joking: "Silence, gentlemen. This is a time for tears not laughter – even for the victors."

He was, nevertheless, justly proud of the day's work and wrote a letter to Henry III, a garbled version of which still exists. In it he said that he regarded the victory of Coutras as "the defeat of the sole enemies of the King and the triumph of those who sought to serve the Crown and his royal person." But he failed to follow up this resounding victory. The Poitou and the Saintonge were now at his mercy. He could have conquered them without any difficulty and then marched on to join up with the German mercenaries. Instead of doing this, however, he left the scene of the battle next morning accompanied only by a small bodyguard of cavalry and galloped along the road to Pau, where his beloved Corisande was in residence at the château, in order to lay the captured standards of the enemy at her feet. In the words of Aubigné, "He threw his words to the wind and gave away his victory to love."

The mere fact that he loved Corisande more than any wife or mistress does not seem to be a sufficient explanation of why, at a time when he could so easily have brought the 'War of the three Kings'* to a satisfactory conclusion he spent the next fourteen months with her in Pau. It has been suggested that it was because he realized that the exploitation of his success at Coutras and joining up with the German Protestants would put him at the head of a victorious army in direct conflict not only with The League but also with the King of France†, and that as the heir presumptive this might be a foolish thing to do. He

* The three kings were Henry III, Henry of Navarre and Henri de Guise.
† See *Henri IV* by Georges Slocombe, (Payot) Paris, 1933.

may have thought that it would help the Protestant cause more if he were to bide his time and, for a while at any rate, rest on his laurels. To do otherwise might be tempting providence. If he were to appear outside the walls of Paris in command of all the Protestant forces it might humiliate Henry III to such an extent as to throw him into the arms of the Guises, which was the last thing that he wanted to happen.

Whatever Henry of Navarre's reason may have been for returning to Pau, its consequences for the Protestant cause were disastrous. The Huguenot army disbanded, even though Condé tried hard to regroup it. It had been arranged that the foreign mercenaries should establish themselves in Lorraine and deal with the Catholics there, which would then have left them free to mop up the Catholics in the south. In much the same way as happened in September 1914 – when the Kaiser's army under von Kluck, which was supposed to outflank the French army north of Paris, suddenly decided to turn south towards the French capital and were defeated at the battle of the Marne – the German invaders on this occasion marched westward towards the Loire with the intention of joining up with the other Hugeunot forces. They were also badly led, as Dohna, who commanded the Germans and the Swiss, although he was experienced, was an extremely poor tactician, and their morale was very low. A mutiny broke out amongst the Swiss army and the other foreign mercenaries who complained that they had no one to lead them as the King of Navarre was dead*. They retreated in confusion to Lorraine, where they were continually harassed by de Guise, who immediately took advantage of the situation.

To make matters worse the Prince de Condé died on 5th March 1588 in most suspicious circumstances. No one doubted that, in fact, he had been poisoned, and the finger of suspicion was pointed to his wife, Charlotte de La Tremouille, whom he had married only two years previously. When the news of this reached the King of Navarre he left Pau and went with all speed to Saint Jean d'Angely, where the Princess de Condé was said to be. This information was correct, and as soon as he arrived there he had her put in prison. On 10th March he wrote to Corisande. "The most terrible thing that I never believed

* This rumour had been spread around by the leaders of the mutiny.

possible has just happened. Monsieur le Prince has just died suddenly and mysteriously." His grief, however, was not shared by The League, whose members were overcome with joy, and Henry III was also not displeased.

Shortly afterwards an attempt was made on the King of Navarre's life. The would-be murderer arrived at Nerac and obtained an audience with Henry, saying that he had brought a message for the King of Navarre. He had a dagger hidden under his doublet, but his courage failed him at the last moment and nothing happened. Later he made a full confession.

Navarre was well aware that other attempts might be made on his life for he wrote to a friend shortly after Condé's death saying that he knew of several people who were ready to kill him at the first opportunity. Nor did he rule out the possibility that he might meet his death by poisoning as his cousin Condé had done, and for some time he refused to sit down to a meal except with people whom he knew well and felt certain he could trust.

Three months before Condé died Guise had returned from his guerilla campaign against the Germans, and the Catholic princes held a reunion at Nancy. They made no secret of the fact that they had formally allied themselves with Philip II of Spain and openly approved his plans to invade England and deal a mortal blow to Queen Elizabeth, to her Church and consequently to Protestantism in Europe. This was the Catholics' grand design. The inhabitants of Lorraine were fully behind it as they had sworn to avenge Mary Stuart and the downfall of Elizabeth would make this possible. The Duc d'Aumale had already captured and occupied the strongest towns in Picardy so that the 'Invincible Armada' could use the Channel ports as an assembly point and as bases for their supplies, and he intended to seize Boulogne, which was considered the best port for such a purpose, but at the first attempt his troops were beaten off by artillery fire.

Henry III was not happy about Philip's intentions and was certainly not prepared to let him use the coasts of Picardy as a base for the invasion of England. When Condé died a new governor of Picardy had to be appointed, so the King chose the Duc de Nevers to succeed him, as Nevers had recently ceased to be a member of The League, and Henry thought he could be trusted faithfully to carry out his orders to protect the Channel ports at all costs.

In April 1588 Henry III opened negotiations with The League at Soissons, but it soon appeared that they would not lead to any satisfactory settlement of the problem. He had in the past when dealing with The League been far too lenient and felt that he could make no more of the concessions which had so far only led to a hardening of attitude on the part of The League. It was while these negotiations were going on that the King heard of a plan which was on foot for Guise and the Duc d'Aumale to enter Paris with a strong force of cavalry. He reinforced his guards and got in touch with the Swiss troops – who had not yet gone back but were in the east of France not far from the Swiss frontier – and arranged for them to move to Paris, where he stationed them in the Faubourg St-Denis.

Meanwhile the members of The League who were not taking part in the Conference at Soissons but had remained in Paris told the Duc de Guise that it was essential that he should return to the capital at once. Despite the extra precautions which the King had taken to defend the city, Guise succeeded in passing through the gates at Denis by pulling his hat well down over his head and hiding the lower part of his face with his cloak. Once inside one of his staff suggested that he should no longer conceal his identity. As soon as he was recognized he was acclaimed by the crowds with the shouts of "Long live Guise, the pillar of the Church – now that you are here we shall all be saved."

His first port of call was a convent in the rue St Honoré, where the Queen Mother, who had not been in good health for some time, was then staying. While she made it quite clear that his visit could have come at a more opportune time, she nevertheless received him politely and offered to take him to the Louvre to see the King. When they arrived, Henry, amazed at Guise's bravado, was furious and asked why he had dared to disobey the King's orders and come to Paris where he was not wanted. There is no record of what went on during the remainder of the short interview, but it is evident that when he left, Guise was more confident than he had been when he arrived at the Louvre.

When he was dismissed by the King from this unforeseen

and unwanted audience, Catherine de Medici, who left with
him, took him to her salon and tried to come to some settlement
about the situation in Picardy, but she met with no success. She
no longer had the same influence or the same force of persuasion
which in the past had so often led to a temporary appeasement
of the Catholics and Protestants.

The atmosphere in Paris was now becoming extremely tense.
The city was full of royalist troops, but at the same time
barricades had been erected in all the principal districts. The
League was now in almost complete control, and it had even
gained the support of several of the King's advisers who had
come to the conclusion that the interests of their country and
even of Henry III himself rested with The League. The King
had made plans to arrest all the Catholic leaders in Paris if he
thought the situation demanded it.

Meanwhile he felt he would be safer out of Paris, and he
succeeded in escaping in the middle of the night through one of
the gates of the city which was not guarded. Avoiding the main
roads he managed to reach Rambouillet without meeting with
any opposition and on the following day took refuge in Chartres.
His mother – who could not have made the journey in any event
for she was crippled with gout – remained behind and made one
last attempt to appease the Duc de Guise by granting the
Catholics further concessions.

During his temporary exile in Chartres Henry III agreed to
call the States General together for the purpose of nominating
a successor to the throne who was of the royal blood but, at
the same time, unlike the heir presumptive, of the Catholic
faith; but before he could do this a delegation of the Paris
bourgeoisie obtained an audience with the King, who was still
in Chartres, and demanded that he should continue the war
against the 'heretics'. The action taken by The League during
the previous few weeks was beginning to turn the tide in the
King's favour. Despite all his faults there were still many who
remained loyal to the monarchy as an institution, if not to the
King himself, and they resented the humiliation to which he
had been subjected by the Leaguers, and particularly the
Guises. As one of them said, "It is a great pity when the valet
dismisses his master." A split became evident in the ranks of the
Catholics themselves, and a party was formed by those who

called themselves 'royal Catholics'. The League began to wonder whether they had gone too far, and even the King of Navarre, from his retreat in the Béarn, proclaimed his loyalty to the rightful King of France by offering to defend him and the Throne should he be called upon to do so and declaring that the Duc de Guise was a usurper. He called upon 'all good Frenchmen' to follow him.

When the bourgeois delegates had left Chartres after the King had agreed to their demands, Henry III sent his doctor to Paris to negotiate with the Leaguers and the Catholic princes on his behalf. The Queen Mother demanded that they should formulate the demands, which they did, and the King agreed to accept nearly all of them, which he ratified by signing an Edict of Union at Rouen in July 1588. This gave The League more power than they had ever had in the past. In addition to further territorial concessions, Henri de Guise was appointed Lieutenant-General of the King's armies, the Cardinal de Bourbon was proclaimed "successor to the throne and first prince of the blood," and the States General were to be convoked in order to 'propose new reforms'. As was usual on these occasions – and there had been many of them since Henry III's accession to the throne – the foundation upon which the edict rested was the 'extirpation of heresy' throughout the whole kingdom.

It is not surprising that, after such an abject surrender as the Edict of Rouen, The League imagined that they had at last got complete control of their vacillating king. They were so confident about it that they decided to show some generosity and went to Chartres to thank him. The Duc de Guise and his brother the Cardinal also condescended to pay him a visit and received a warm welcome. The King appeared to have accepted his defeat with fortitude, but secretly he was preparing to get his revenge. He distrusted his mother, who wanted him to effect a reconciliation with the 'victors of the barricade,' and he never forgave his ministers, who had advised him to come to terms with The League.

On 16th August 1588 the States General met at Blois, where the King had established his court and his government. A large majority of its members had by then transferred their allegiance to Henri de Guise, and the States General proceeded to make some revolutionary changes in the constitution, which left the King little more than a puppet on a string with Guise calling the tune, and he was faced by what was described as "a pack of hounds out for blood." The time to strike had come.

On 22nd December he let it be known that on the following day he intended to go to La Noue, a house not far from Blois, and would preside over his Council of Ministers before he left. The same evening, under the pretext of making certain preparations for the move on the following morning, he handed over the keys of the château for safe keeping and spent the night on the second floor in the wing which had been built by Francis I. His Council of Ministers arrived early in the morning, and most of them had already been secretly informed of the King's intention, which was to get rid of his greatest enemy once and for all. Henry had entrusted this mission to an organization known as the 'Forty Five', who were fanatical opponents of The League. He issued them with daggers and posted eight of them in his room and the others in a small room adjacent to it and in the corridor which led from the King's room to the top of the staircase, where they all waited for Henri de Guise to arrive.

Guise had been warned on more than one occasion by his friends that the King had designs on his life, but he refused to believe it, saying, "He would never dare." Nevertheless, a sense of danger was in the air. The Papal Nuncio, who was attached to Guise's staff, had urged him not to remain at Blois, and his mother, the Duchesse de Nemours, had begged her son to leave. Even Catherine de Medici, who had more than an inkling of what was going to happen, would have warned him of the danger had she not thought that it would be betraying her son. At 7 a.m. on the morning of the 23rd December Guise was informed that the Council of Ministers was assembling, and the King, who was watching from the window of his room, saw Monsieur le Duc arrive in company with the Cardinal de Guise. Henry was in a state of great excitement and could not keep still and sent one of his equerries to ask his chaplain, Dourguin, to pray for the success of the operation which was going to bring peace to his kingdom.

When the Duc de Guise reached the foot of the staircase which led up to the door of the Council Chamber he was surprised to

(*left*) Charles, Duc de Mayenne. (*right*) Henri, Duc de Guise

The assassination of the Guise brothers on the orders of Henry III, guided by the 'diabolic' advice of d'Epernon

The assassination of Henry III by Jacques Clement

see the archers of the royal guard posted there under the command of Captain Larchant. Larchant put his mind at rest, however, by telling Guise that "these poor men" were presenting a petition to the council for more pay and had come there to ask him to intercede on their behalf. Guise promised to do so and went upstairs. The Cardinal de Guise and the Archbishop of Lyons then arrived, and the Council began its business.

While they were still dealing with the first subject on the agenda Revol, a Secretary of State, approached Guise and told him in a whisper that His Majesty wanted to see him in his room immediately. Guise left the Council chamber and was shown the way to the King's room, where the Court usher announced him and then shut the door. When he entered he came face to face with the 'Forty-Five', who saluted him. He turned round and tried to run away, but the murder squad, for that was what they were, seized him by the arms and legs and stabbed him with their daggers. He fell, mortally wounded, at the foot of the King's bed.

The Cardinal and the Archbishop were arrested, and both thrown into prison, where they remained until the following morning when one of the officers of the King's guard led the Cardinal outside under the pretext that the King wanted to see him. He had not gone more than a dozen paces from the prison door when he was set upon by soldiers of the guard, who killed him with their pikes. The bodies of the two Guises were burned and their ashes thrown into the river Loire.

Henry III was delighted with the day's work, but when the Queen Mother, who was lying on her deathbed, heard the news she was appalled.

"What have you done?" she exclaimed.

"Now I am King of France," he said. "I have killed the King of Paris."

"God grant it may be so," was her reply, "but have you made sure of the other towns?"

Two weeks later she was dead. Knowing full well the consequences that would follow the assassination of Guise she had no wish to go on living. She had certainly had her fill of sorrow during her life. At a time when France needed a firm, wise and tolerant king the throne had been occupied by three of the weakest kings in the whole of its history, Catherine's three sons,

Francis II, Charles IX and Henry III. The first was a permanent invalid, the second was mentally unbalanced, and the
third a degenerate. She did her best to support them but failed
miserably. Her greatest handicap was perhaps that she was a
'woman and an alien'*. She tried hard to preserve the balance
between Catholic and Protestant, but all she succeeded in doing
was to antagonize them both. When she died the situation was
at its worst, and she must have known that her son Henry's days
were numbered.†

However, the King was not satisfied with having got rid of
both the Guises. He proceeded to have all the Leaguers and
the princes of the house of Lorraine who were in Blois arrested
and thrown into prison, but neither this nor the Blois murderers
wrecked The League as Henry had hoped. The massacre of St
Bartholomew did not put an end to the 'Protestant Cause' in
France, and The League was strengthened by the King's rash
action rather than weakened, but only temporarily.

The whole of Paris rose as one man against him, and he was
from then on referred to as 'Henry III, the late King of
France'. The League itself refused to have any dealings with
Monsieur Henri de Valois, as they called him, and regarded the
Cardinal de Bourbon as their monarch. Henry III was now a
king without a throne. It was almost a week before the news of
the murder of the Guises reached Henry of Navarre. He showed
no signs of pleasure and said that if the Duc de Guise had fallen
into his hands he would have been treated differently. At the
same time he realized that with Guise out of the way his
position as heir presumptive to the throne of France was
stronger than ever before, and within the next few days three
more towns surrendered to the Protestant forces: Niort, St
Maixent and Maillezais.

In a letter to Corisande telling her the exciting news he wrote,
"I can hardly wait to be able to tell you that someone has been
sent to strangle the Queen of Navarre: that and the death of her
mother* would make me sing the hymn of Simeon."‡

The new successful campaign of Navarre's army was tem-

* See *History of Europe*, by H. A. L. Fisher.

† This letter was written on 1st January 1589 only four days before the
Queen Mother died.

‡ The *Nunc Dimittis*.

porarily brought to a halt a few days later by his suddenly being taken ill. It was a very cold winter, he caught a severe chill, and for a few days his life was in danger. Had he died then, the whole history of France would have changed, and it is difficult to imagine what would have happened. In all probability the French Revolution would have been brought forward 200 years, for never had the monarchy been in such disrepute.

His illness, severe though it was, did not last long, however, and by 10th January he was out of danger. "My dearest heart," he wrote to Corisande, "I have seen the heavens open but I was not good enough to be allowed to enter. God still has need of my services."

As soon as he was fit again the King of Navarre resumed command of his army and captured four more towns, including Chatellerault, whence he issued his famous proclamation offering his hand to the King of France and calling on all Frenchmen to unite for the cause of tolerance and peace. "We are in a house which is about to collapse; in a ship about to sink. I demand unity in the name of us all, for my King, for myself, for all Frenchmen and for France herself."

The wording of the proclamation concisely expressed his innermost thoughts and his intentions when in the near future, as seemed most probable, he became Henry IV, King of France. He realized the state to which the Wars of Religion had brought the country and the importance of putting an end to the internecine strife between the Catholics and Protestants. He cared for the common people of France and wished to see them prosperous and happy. When he became king he was determined that they should be.

After the capture of Chatellerault and the King of Navarre's appeal to the nation, Henry III had no alternative but to come to terms with the Protestants, and he sent the Duchesse d'Angouleme to his brother-in-law to urge him to effect a reconciliation. On 30th April the King of Navarre arrived at Plessis-les-Tours, where negotiations between the two kings were opened. Navarre promised 'on his honour' that he would never deny the Catholics freedom of worship and liberty of conscience and that he wished for nothing better than a re-conciliation with his King. Henry, for his part, issued a proc-lamation formally revoking the edict by which the States

General at Blois five months previously had disinherited Navarre from the succession.

The two armies being now under the same command, the King established himself at St Cloud, while Henry of Navarre advanced towards Paris and on 30th July began surrounding the city, which was in a state of turmoil. The Parisians' hatred of their King had reached boiling point, and delirious crowds paraded in the streets day and night. The King's portraits, which hung in the Louvre, were mutilated, and the parish priests cast spells on him at the altars of their churches. Bands of children carrying candles marched up and down the boulevards shouting, "Stamp out the House of Valois." The news of the successes of the royalist and Huguenot armies raised the atmosphere to fever pitch, and the rumour went round that the King had told Madame de Montpensier* that as soon as he entered the city he would burn her alive. No one knew what was going to happen.

One of the most fanatical supporters of The League was a young monk, Jacques Clement, born in the village of Sorbonne near Sens. He was the son of simple peasants and talked so often about leading a revolution that his friends had given him the nickname of 'Le Capitaine'. He approached a doctor, whom he knew and trusted, and asked him whether it was legally justifiable to murder a tyrant and was apparently given an answer that put his tortured mind, such as it was, at rest. He was, however, mentally unbalanced and was just the right person to choose as a hired assassin, for if, in fact, he did murder the King it would naturally be assumed that he was not legally responsible for the crime because of his insanity. What better agent could be found to get rid of a king who had been responsible for the murder of the Guises? It is not definitely known who was behind it all, but there is some evidence, including a remark she made when she heard the news of the King's death, that Madame de Montpensier had something to do with it.

It is certainly known, however, that Clement was given a forged letter purporting to have been written and signed by Achille de Harlay, who was a prisoner in the Bastille and an opponent of The League, asking for an audience with his

* The Duchesse de Montpensier, sister of Henri de Guise and a great supporter of The League.

Majesty. The Comte de Brissac, who was detained in the Louvre also provided him with a pass which would enable him to get through the troops who were guarding the King at St Cloud. There was really no need for this as the monk's habit which he wore was sufficient to ensure his safe passage through the royalist lines.

When Clement arrived at St Cloud on the evening of 31st July 1589 he was taken to see La Guesle, who was the King's Procureur General.* He told La Guesle that he wished to see His Majesty on a matter of great importance and was told that this would not be possible until the following morning, but if he wished he could spend the night in the château.

He spent quite an enjoyable evening drinking and eating in the servants hall and cut his meat up with a long knife with a black handle, which he produced from under his habit. No one, however, seems to have regarded this with any suspicion. Among other things he talked about the growing anger of the monks against the King who had betrayed the Catholics and made so many concessions to the Huguenots.

The following morning at 7 a.m. the Procureur General took Clement to the royal apartment, where the King was sitting on his 'chaise'†, looking very scruffy and still in his night-shirt, having just got out of bed. Nevertheless, Clement was admitted, and when he had been presented to the King he bowed and asked whether he might speak to His Majesty in private because the purpose of his visit was confidential. Henry, who strangely enough suspected nothing, told La Guesle to leave. As soon as they were left alone Clement took the knife which was hidden up his sleeve and stabbed the King just below the navel. The King uttered a cry, and La Guesle, who had been waiting outside, rushed into the room with drawn sword. Clement was standing there with his arms extended in the shape of a cross and waiting. The guards outside the King's room then entered and killed him. When the royal physician arrived he did not think that the King's wound was a mortal one, but by the evening his condition had become much more serious. He had

* Attorney-General.
† In the only existing account of the murder, the word *chaise* (chair) is in inverted commas, from which it is natural to assume that this was a euphemism for night-commode.

developed violent pains in his intestines and had frequent bouts of fainting.

Henry of Navarre, who was still at Meudon, which was only a few kilometres away, was immediately sent for, but by the time he arrived the King was *in extremis*, although he was able to embrace him. He also acknowledged his brother-in-law as the rightful heir to the throne but begged him to abjure the Protestant faith and become a Catholic. Just before he died he sent for the noblemen of his court and commanded them as their King to be loyal to his successor. They promised to do so. A few hours later the King was dead.

6 The new King

NEXT day Henry IV, as he now was, noticed a great change in the attitude of the nobles. They were appalled at the prospect of a Protestant king on the throne of France. "Better no King than a Huguenot," they said. But they were not all in agreement as to what was the proper line to adopt. The extremists wanted to come out into the open and refuse to accept him as the rightful king of France. More moderate counsel prevailed, however, and a delegation was appointed to see the King and demand that before they recognized him he should follow Henry III's advice and be converted to Catholicism.

Henry IV had no illusions about the precarious position he was in and realized how difficult it was going to be for a Protestant King to govern a country in which a large majority of his subjects were Catholics. He had changed his religion twice before, and he saw that eventually it might become inevitable that he should do so again; but before he came to any decision he had to consider the arguments for and against. To abjure the Protestant faith would, in all probability, mean losing many supporters and not only in his own kingdom. It might well alienate the 'reformers' in England, Germany and Switzerland, who had been his allies for some years. Nor was he by any means sure that changing his denomination would win over The League to his side, as they did not want him as king whatever his religious persuasion might be. He therefore decided to postpone taking any action until such time as he could establish religious tolerance throughout the kingdom. This he was determined to do, by persuasion if possible but by force if necessary. However, he was already convinced as he was to say later, that Paris was worth a Mass.

It was essential, therefore, that something should be done,

and done quickly, to convince his subjects that after thirty years of weak government, strong measures were necessary to pull the country together. Accordingly, on 4th August, only three days after his accession to the throne, he issued a proclamation setting out his policy with the object of satisfying his friends and supporters and, at the same time, pacifying his enemies. In it he promised to maintain the Catholic Apotolic Church of Rome in its entirety and as the chief religious body in the realm; to submit the question of his own religion so the decision of a 'free Council', which he proposed to convoke in six months' time. As for the Calvinists, they would retaitn their right to freedom of worship in the towns which they at present held under the various edicts signed by Henry III, but the places which had been acquired by force of arms would have to be handed back to 'our good Catholic subjects'.

The proclamation immediately produced one concrete result, for most of the dukes, peers, and high officials of the Crown who had met at St Cloud twenty-four hours after Henry III had been murdered and had delivered an ultimatum to the new King, decided "in view of the solemn promises which he had just made, to recognize him as their King according to the law and of the Kingdom". They also promised to serve and obey him and undertook to support him "with their possessions and their lives in subduing the rebels and enemies who wished to undermine the State".

There were still many people, however, who were not prepared to accept him unconditionally as king. One of them was Thomas de Verdun, the Advocate General of Caen, who declared that he accepted the heir presumptive as his king for the time being, but if by the end of six months Henry had not become a Catholic he would no longer do so.

There was also further opposition from the Protestants themselves. In the Poitou and Gascony, where many of Henry's most fervid supporters were previously to be found, they refused to obey "a perjurer who had promised to maintain papist idolatry", and many of them deserted from Henry's army and returned to their towns and villages to run their businesses, or tend their crops. Because of this the King's large army of some 40,000 men was reduced to about 22,000. Nor was this all. Most of the principal towns in France stood steadfastly behind

The League, and only Tours, Bordeaux, Langres, Chalons, Compiegne and Clermont-Ferrand remained loyal to him.

Not more than a sixth of France at the most optimistic estimate was loyal to the new King, and with his army reduced in strength by little less than 50 per cent, the general situation was not very encouraging. Some of his military advisers thought that the King ought to withdraw his forces south of the Loire, but he would not hear of it and doubtless, agreed with Givry, who had said when the suggestion was made, "Who would believe that you were the King of France if your orders were issued from Limoges?"

In any event he was convinced that he would not improve his position by retreating and that the best way of conquering the whole of his kingdom would be to capture Paris. Once he had Paris under his control he felt that the rest would not be difficult. Paris was the stronghold of The League, to destroy which was his main objective.

As soon as the news of Henry III's death reached them, the Duchesses de Nemours and de Montpensier spread the story of what they called "the heroic act of Jacques Clement" all over Paris, and the inhabitants of the capital celebrated the occasion for many days and nights. However, the royalists, although they had little liking for the late king, had still less for his successor, the Huguenot prince. It was for this reason that the Duc de Mayenne, who had succeeded Henri de Guise as head of The League proclaimed the Cardinal de Bourbon king under the name of Charles X. It was not a clever move, however, for, apart from being old, the Cardinal was powerless as he was a prisoner of Henry IV.

Meanwhile the King, realizing that to attack Paris with his reduced army was out of the question, decided to split it up into three army corps, one of which was sent to the Champagne, another to Picardy and the third to Normandy. This made the army more mobile and enabled him to make a show of force in several regions at the same time.

The two corps allotted to the Champagne and Picardy were commanded respectively by the Maréchal Aumont and the Duc de Longueville, while the King commanded the third. On 8th August, for he had no time to lose, Henry left Meudon and advanced towards Normandy with 700 cavalry and 4,000

infantry. His intention was to set up a base in Dieppe, where he
would be able to receive reinforcements from England should
they be available. Furthermore the governor of Dieppe, de
Chaste, who was openly on the side of the King, had promised
to give him control of the port. After marching for twelve days
he reached Dieppe, which opened its gates to him, and he told
the inhabitants that all he wanted from them was "their
friendship, good bread, good wine and hospitality." As soon as
the news that the King had left Meudon reached Mayenne he
set off in pursuit.

Having established a base for military operations, Henry
took up a carefully prepared position to meet any attack from
the armed forces of The League, which he rightly expected
would not be long delayed. After a thorough reconnaissance
Henry decided that the best tactical position from which he
could meet an attack from Mayenne's army, which was three
times the strength of his own, was in a triangular valley formed
by two small rivers, the Eaulne and the Bethune, which was
dominated by the Château d'Arques and was only a few kilometres from the outskirts of Dieppe. The side facing the enemy
was covered with thick woodlands and protected by trenches.

On 16th September Mayenne's advance guard had its first
skirmishes with the King's infantry, during which one of
Mayenne's officers was taken prisoner and brought before the
King. He seemed very confident and told the King that in a few
hours the position would be attacked by a large force and that
he could not see enough of the King's troops capable of putting
up any resistance, to which Henry replied, "What you can see
is not everything. You have forgotten that I have God on my side."

During the night of 20th/21st September, Mayenne's forces
entered the valley under cover of a heavy mist, and on the
following morning at dawn attacked Henry's main position.
The battle went on for almost a fortnight, and for some time
Mayenne's troops gained ground, although several attacks were
beaten off with heavy casualties. The mist had continued for
several days, and the King's artillery had been unable to go
into action, but finally it cleared, and Mayenne was forced to
withdraw. Unable to take the position by a frontal attack,
he tried several times to turn it by attacking both flanks,
but on 6th October he gave it up and retired in disorder.

Having reorganized his army, he marched towards Dieppe along the left bank of the river Bethune but failed to take the town. Henry had been reinforced by English and Scottish troops and the Maréchal d'Aumont and the Duc de Longueville had joined forces and were already on their way to reinforce the King. Frightened of being caught between the two armies, Mayenne retreated in the direction of Paris.

The King's victory was celebrated in Arques, where the Catholics sang a Te Deum and the Huguenots their psalms, for the royal forces were composed of both denominations – which boded well for the future. Differences in religious beliefs are forgotten when men are fighting together for the same cause. It was obviously with this in mind that the King addressed his troops after the battle was over.

"We all believe in the same God," he told them. "Each of us hopes for eternal glory through the grace of Jesus Christ, but we have different ways of obtaining it. You pray in your way and I will pray in mine."

Having at least temporarily dealt with the position in Normandy, the King thought that an attack on Paris might be successful now that he had received substantial reinforcements from abroad, and he therefore marched towards the capital. By the end of October he had managed to establish his troops in three villages on the outskirts of Paris without Mayenne having learned of his approach. On the morning of 1st November they attacked the suburbs on the left bank of the Seine, and before midday they had taken the trenches manned by The Leaguers. They then continued their advance as far as the city walls and occupied the Abbey at St Germain-des-Pres but were not able to push forward any further and failed to enter Paris itself. Henry gave orders for his infantry to take up positions ready for a new assault, but on 3rd November decided that it would not yet be possible to take the city without a long siege for which his army was not yet fully prepared.

The attack on St Germain, though partially successful, had most unfortunate repercussions and rekindled the Parisian's hatred for their king, which was just beginning to die down. Some years previously, remembering his personal experience when he was still a young boy of the atrocities committed by Condé's army in the Languedoc and Gascony, Henry had warned his troops before they attacked Agen that he would deal severely with anyone who did not comply with the civilized rules of warfare. Believing that they were attacking Paris to avenge the massacre of St Bartholomew, which, not unnaturally, was something they could never forget, his Huguenot soldiers killed 400 unarmed civilians in St Germain, an act which The League did not fail to use as anti-Huguenot propaganda. This did Henry and the Protestant cause untold harm.

Having retreated from Paris the King took up winter quarters in Tours, where he arrived on 21st November and from where he was able to keep an eye on the neighbouring provinces. He did not spend the winter months doing nothing but made several expeditions and occupied many towns including Le Mans, Bourges, Orleans and Vendôme.

The first of these, Le Mans, he reached on 27th November, only six days after his army had arrived in Tours, so he had not wasted much time. The town was held by the Leaguers and the governor, Bois Dauphin, only had about one hundred armed men to defend it. When called upon to open the gates he bravely but rashly refused and said that his men would open fire on the royalist troops should they attempt to force an entry. Henry, in order to spare the town's inhabitants, ordered his troops not to advance but later Bois Dauphin changed his mind and let them in.

From Le Mans the King went on to Laval, where he was acclaimed by the whole population including the Catholic clergy, which was a welcome sign of the times, for it was gradually becoming clear that in provincial France The League was losing many former supporters who were beginning to realize that eventually their king would win the struggle to unite his kingdom.

While he was still waiting for spring to come before returning to Normandy, Henry set up his government in Tours, and before he left Achille de Harlay joined him with all the other loyal magistrates who had escaped with him from the Bastille, where they had been imprisoned by Henry III. Both the King and the Leaguers had a parliament of their own in almost every province, as, for example, in Normandy, where the King's was in Caen and The Leaguers' in Rouen.

In Tours which was, as has already been mentioned, during the winter of 1589–90 the seat of Henry IV's government, his position had been considerably strengthened by the decision of the Senate of Venice to send an Ambassador accredited to the King of France. The new Ambassador, Jean Mocenigo, was received in audience by Henry and congratulated him on his accession to the throne. He also reminded him of the treaties between their two countries. The Venetian Senate doubtless hoped that good relations between themselves and the French King might influence his decision regarding his abjuration of the Protestant faith which he had promised to make within six months of his accession, but he was not yet ready to do this. He was not over anxious in any event to change his religion again, as he had already done so on two previous occasions, but now he had another reason for remaining a Protestant. During the last four months he had won a number of victories on the field of battle, and this had given him greater confidence. There was a distinct chance that he might subdue his rebellious subjects by force of arms, in which event it might not be necessary to sell his soul in order to save his kingdom and his throne.

The council which he had promised at St Cloud to convoke to settle the question of his religious status was due to assemble at the end of January 1590, but the King decided to postpone the date until 15th March and issued a proclamation to this effect.

Before the winter was over Henry IV had drawn up a plan of operations which he hoped would open the way to a final and decisive attack on Paris before the end of the year. He intended to entice Mayenne to leave Paris and then attack him. Having then defeated The League's army, he would march on Paris, which was his main objective. About the middle of February 1590, therefore, in accordance with his plan of battle, he marched into Normandy via Le Mans and Alençon and captured the strongly fortified château in the latter town with scarcely a shot being fired. From there he went to Sees and Argentan, both of which he occupied without any difficulty, and eventually appeared before the walls of Falaise. The château of Falaise, which was built on a large rock which completely dominated the town, was surrounded by deep moats and strongly defended, but the King's troops breeched the walls and

forced Brissac to surrender. Next day he continued to march in
a northerly direction towards Caen and the coast and at Lisieux
had another great success. As he himself wrote, "I took the
place without firing one of my canons, except to make fun of
them, yet it was defended by a thousand men and thirty
officers." By the end of January practically the whole of Normandy was under the King's control, and the only town still
held by The League was Rouen.

When he heard the news of the King's successful campaign
in Normandy, Mayenne – who had again been reinforced and
now had an army of 20,000, including 8,000 cavalry – left Paris
and marched in a north-westerly direction to Meulan, capturing Vincennes and Pontoise on the way. The King, who had
surrounded Dreux and was about to attack, it turned north-
east and tried to turn the enemy's flank, but Mayenne did not
want to be drawn into battle so soon, and withdrew from
Meulan toward Poissy.

The two armies met on the plain of Ivry, which lies between
Mantes and Dreux, and Henry, who knew of Mayenne's withdrawal from Meulan, was already there and had been waiting
for him since 11th March at St André where Mayenne's army
had just crossed the river Eure. The royalist army was by then
in touch with the enemy, who could not retreat as they had the
river behind them, and they had no alternative but to fight.

On the morning of 14th March the King's army was drawn
up in the following formation. In the centre was the bulk of his
cavalry, commanded by him, and on each flank were the infantry composed of French, Germans and Swiss, commanded
respectively by Maréchal d'Aumont and the Duc de Montpensier. In reserve was the remainder of the infantry under
Maréchal Biron. Mayenne's troops were drawn up much in
the same way, his cavalry in the centre and the infantry on
either flank. The fighting lasted for no longer than one hour and
no battle was ever won so decisively.

Just before he gave orders for the cavalry to charge the King
addressed his troops in words which have since become as
famous as the speech made by Henry V of England before the
walls of Harfleur.* "Comrades," he said, "God is with us. Here

* "Once more into the breach, dear friends, once more; Or close the
wall up with our English dead!

are his enemies and ours. Here is your King. Advance towards
them and if you lose your standards follow my white plumes
and you will find the way to honour and glory." More than
once in the thick of the battle at the head of his troops the white
plumes on his helmet could be seen as he led the charging
cavalry*. The League's mercenaries had already suffered
heavy casualties from artillery fire, and when the King's cavalry
charged they retreated in disorder.

It was a shattering defeat for Mayenne, and he freely admitted it in a letter to the King of Spain.

> The desperate charge made by the enemy [he wrote] so took my
> squadrons by surprise that most of them in less than an hour
> abandoned the field of battle leaving me with less than seven
> squadrons of cavalry all of whom, I can assure your Majesty were
> killed, wounded or taken prisoner.

As for the King he gave a graphic account of the battle in a
letter which he sent to the Duc de Longueville that same night.

> My Cousin, [he wrote] we must thank God for he has given us a
> fine victory. When the battle started things began to move quickly,
> and God in his wisdom determined the outcome. The infantry,
> foreign as well as the French, surrendered and the retreating
> troops were pursued to the gates of Mantes. I can rightly say that
> I was well served but above all God gave me his help and proved
> to my enemies that he minds not small or large victories. I will
> despatch details at the first opportunity. Your brother showed,
> like myself that he has little fear of the Spaniards. He did very
> well . . . my courier reports that the Duc de Mayenne has retreated
> to Mantes. Believe it, my Cousin it is peace in my Kingdom and
> the destruction of The League which all good Frenchmen must
> strive to obtain.

March 14th was a bad day for The League, for they suffered
another defeat in the Auvergne when the Comte de Randan,
who was the governor of the province appointed by The League,
was defeated, and the royalists gained control of the whole
province.

* The King's *panaches blancs*' (white plumes) were not a myth. Accounts of
the Treasury of Navarre give the date on which they were acquired and the
price, which was 100 écus.

The retreat of the army of The League in the direction of
Picardy opened the way for the King's next move, which was
to march on Paris. On 15th March he entered Mantes, but
instead of moving on immediately, he stayed there until the
end of the month and did not put in an appearance before the
gates of Paris until 7th May. Many explanations have been
given of this long delay, including one given by Sully, who said
that the King stayed at Mantes because he wanted to go hunting. Knowing his fondness for the chase, such an explanation
was not unbelievable, but this was not the real reason for not
pushing on at once. The twelve days spent in Mantes were no
longer than was necessary to supply, re-equip and regroup his
army for the siege of Paris, by which he hoped to end the war. He
was expecting to receive in the near future a new supply of
ammunition from England, and in addition to this the weather
had taken a turn for the worse. There had been torrential rain
and floods were widespread. Meanwhile the news of the King's
great victory at Ivry had raised a storm in Paris. The League's
executive committee known as 'Les Seize'*, were the first to
hear about it, and they were extremely worried, for they
thought that there might be a dramatic change of public
opinion which would result in their losing many supporters, for
'nothing succeeds like success'. After the first shock was over,
however, the people of Paris quickly recovered and would not
listen to any suggestion that perhaps it might be wise to come to
terms with the King. A number of people who advised negotiating were thrown into the Seine for their temerity.

The twelve days rest which Henry had given his army in
Mantes gave him time to think very carefully about his plan
for besieging Paris. As soon as his supply of ammunition arrived,
however, he began his march on the capital, capturing a
number of places on the way, including Melun, Bray-sur-Seine
and Montereau. Within a few weeks all the well-defended
towns in the environs of Paris were in his hands, and on 7th
May his army was at its gates.

But the Leaguers had not been wasting time since the battle
of Ivry. They had appointed the Duc de Nemours as the new
governor of Paris in place of his brother, reinforced the garrison
with Swiss and German mercenaries, and a *milice* was formed

* The Sixteen.

L'homme a quelque grandeur quil puisse paruenir Las! nous le voyons bien! Entre nous depernon: Combien ceste grand' trouppe & armee furieuse,
Soit par leffort des Armes, ou par fuceffion, Du gaftz, & de Larchant, a la Mort dun tel Roy, Par laquelle efperoit, foubz boulleuerfer Paris,
De mourir chacun iour, il luy fault fouuenir, Qui tant fe promettoit, d'efleuer noftre nom, L'accompagnant fera, grandemant doulloureufe!
Et que fubict Il eft, à Putrefaction. Nous ne luy fçauriōs moins, quapreffer vng charoy En pleurs fe font changes Leurs defefperes Ris,
Parquoy durant letemps, Dvne tant briefue vié, Et tous fes officiers, le conduire à Puiffy, Et ce Roy Nauarrois qui le maine à compiegne,
A employer fes Ans à bien faire ayt enuie. Auec Dueil, Pleurs, et Larmes, ayns le cœur tranfy Preine exemple fur luy qu'ainfi ne luyen preigne.

Henry IV accompanying the corpse of Henry III to Poissy

A gathering of The League to oppose Henry IV

Henry IV abjuring the Protestant faith at St Denis

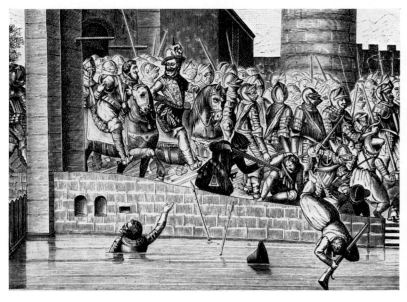

Henry IV's entry into Paris

and armed to guard the city walls.* When the siege began, therefore, a city of 220,000 inhabitants was defended by a garrison numbering 50,000. The King's army, however, only consisted of 13,000 at the most.

There was little point, therefore, in attacking Paris, although an assault was made on the suburb of St Martin, which was unsuccessful, and the attacking troops suffered quite heavy casualties. This only proved what the King already knew – though he wanted confirmation of it – that it was quite out of the question that with such a small army he could possibly capture a city which was defended by almost the entire adult population. He decided that the only way to conquer Paris was to cut off all supplies by a prolonged seige.

This minor victory of the Parisians raised their morale, and everything was done by the Catholic leaders to exacerbate religious hatred. It was God who had given them the victory, they were told, and they must now face the blockade courageously in order to defend the Catholic faith and stamp out Protestant heresy. Two days after the unsuccessful attack on St Martin a spectacular parade of the 'ecclesiastic forces' was held to celebrate the victory. Many thousands of clergy and monks of every order took part, headed by the Bishop of Senlis. As they marched past the papal legate he blessed them. It was a great occasion marred only by one unfortunate incident. Some of the militia wanted to fire a salvo in honour of the Pope's representative, but so inexperienced were they in the use of firearms that all they succeeded in doing was to kill one of his entourage and a servant of the Spanish Ambassador. Anti-Huguenot propaganda was the order of the day from now on and was encouraged by the governor of Paris, the Spanish Ambassador, Mendoza and Cardinal de Bourbon, the Pretender to the French throne.

It was not long, however, before the blockade, although it was not complete, began to have its effect. Within a few days bread was almost unobtainable. The King's one and only hope was to force the Parisians to surrender by starvation, and he stationed some of his troops round Lagny, Charenton and Cor-

---

* The English word for *milice* is militia. The *milice* of Paris were somewhat similar to the Home Guard which was formed in Great Britain when a German invasion was expected in 1940.

beil, through which most of the city's food supplies were daily transported from the provinces of Burgundy and Beauce. He also occupied all the mills so that the wheat was left rotting in the fields where it grew. With the shortage of bread other food had to be found, and, as in the case of many other sieges, dogs, cats and rats became the principal diet until they, too, were in short supply. But that was not the end of it. According to a contemporary chronicler the starving population of Paris dug up the bones of dead bodies in the cemetery to make a substitute for flour and, when it was available even ate human flesh. One woman whose child had died preserved the body in salt, and she and her servant lived on it for several weeks.

The blockade had only been going on for two months when Henry IV, who was sorry for the ordinary Parisians whom he did not consider personally responsible for the city's resistance, announced that anyone who wanted to leave the city might do so. More than 100,000 of them availed themselves of the opportunity, but there were still another 100,000 mouths to feed. This humane gesture on the King's part doubtless greatly helped the governor of Paris, for those who remained consisted mostly of the army, the militia and the other armed civilians, so none of the food was wasted. When the Queen heard of this she sent a letter to her husband. It was the first sign of life she had given since she had begun her forced retreat in the Château d'Usson. "If you had not allowed so many of the besieged to leave Paris," she wrote, "the city would have been forced to surrender. I am astounded that you should have been persuaded to take such a risk."

Nevertheless, although the King was kind and generous by nature, he was foresighted enough to think that his gesture might eventually bear fruit. It was not only his throne that he was trying to save. He wanted to rule over a united nation and to show mercy to the people of Paris might well persuade others that he had the welfare of all his subjects at heart.

The Leaguers thought that this was an opportune moment to open negotiations with the King, as it would show the Parisians, who were now in dire straits, that their leaders were not so intolerant and intransigent as they might appear to be, and should the negotiations break down the blame could be put fairly and squarely on the King.

A delegation, consisting of the Archbishops of Paris and Lyons, was sent to meet the King at the Abbey of St Antoine-des-Champs to suggest that he should discuss with the Duc de Mayenne the terms upon which the pacification of his kingdom could be obtained. Henry received them in audience, and, after listening to all they had to say he gave them the following reply.

> If in order to win a battle I give a finger of my hand I would give two for world peace. I love my town of Paris, she is my eldest daughter. I want to show her more mercy than she asks for, but wish her to owe it to my clemency and not to that of the Duc de Mayenne or the King of Spain. I want to postpone the surrendering of Paris until peace is concluded and this cannot be achieved without many discussions which will take a long time. My city of Paris cannot wait all that time without a lot of suffering. So many people have already died of hunger that if ten or twelve days more were to pass 10,000 or 20,000 more would die and this would be terrible. I am a real father to my people and I would prefer not to have Paris rather than have it ruined and devastated by the death of so many.

Whatever pity he may have felt for the people of Paris, however, the King was well aware that the only reason why the two Archbishops had been sent to him as envoys from The League was that there was really no alternative. The situation in the capital had become desperate. The Parisians were in a state of revolt because while they got less and less food every day the chiefs of The League, the rich bourgeoisie, and the merchants who supplied them always seemed to have plenty. The privileged were in no danger of starving. On 8th August the mob had demonstrated outside the Parliament House shouting, *"Pain ou Paix."**

The Archbishops were, therefore, given an ultimatum. If in a week's time they had not received a reply from Mayenne, Paris must surrender. They agreed to this condition, but asked that the period of grace should not start until Mayenne had been informed of the King's terms. Their request having been granted, they returned to Paris to report the result of their meeting to the Duc de Nemours.

The next few days were terrible; even the army was on the

* Bread or peace.

verge of starvation, and the German mercenaries, resorting to cannibalism, killed some young children and ate them. On 28th August, Paris would have been obliged to surrender within twenty-four hours when suddenly the news arrived that relief was near at hand, The Duke of Parma† acting under orders from Philip II of Spain had withdrawn the Spanish army from the Low Countries, where he was engaged in suppressing a revolt against the Spaniards. After crossing the French frontier he marched towards Paris and joined up with Mayenne at Meaux, which is on the river Marne about forty miles east of Paris, where the head of The League had been reorganizing his army after its defeat by the King at the battle of Ivry. When Henry IV heard that the relieving army was marching on Paris he immediately raised the siege and moved eastward to try and intercept it.

However, the Duke of Parma, who knew that it was a matter of urgency that he should reach Paris quickly and relieve the garrison before it had to surrender, managed to avoid being drawn into battle. He crossed the Marne at Chelles, and, before the King could cut him off, captured Lagny, Charenton and Corbeil, thus opening the road for supplies of food once again to enter Paris without let or hindrance. On 17th September 1590 Mayenne entered the city and the siege was over. Paris was, therefore, saved, but 13,000 of its population had died of starvation, and another 30,000 had been killed by the plague.

Describing the last few weeks of the siege, a member of the papal legate's staff, the Bishop of Asti, wrote, "They had no meat, no fish, no milk, no vegetables, no fruit and practically no bread. I could almost say that there was no sun, no sky and no air. . . . It was a miracle that the city survived."

The relief of Paris was a stunning blow for the King. All the victories of the past twelve months had been in vain, and he was virtually back where he had started.

† In French Duc de Parma, in Italian Ducca di Parma.

7 Three difficult years

HENRY did not know the meaning of despair and was not the man to sit down under defeat. His tough upbringing among the peasants of the Béarn, his powers of leadership, his trying apprenticeship at the Louvre under the eagle eye of Catherine de Medici, the machinations of his two brothers-in-law, Charles IX and Henry III, and his sense of humour were to stand him in good stead during the next three years, which, difficult though they were, ended triumphantly.

Nevertheless, as he took stock of the position in the autumn of 1590, his future prospects cannot have seemed anything but gloomy, for he was, according to his own description, "a king without a kingdom, a husband without a wife and a general without money." Already at the age of only 37 his hair and beard were beginning to turn grey, but otherwise he still retained his youthful vitality, and his energy was boundless. He was said to spend less time in bed than his portly adversary the Duc de Mayenne spent at the table.

Although he had had no alternative but to raise the siege of Paris, and even after the withdrawal of the Duke of Parma had no intention of resuming it, he reoccupied Lagny, Charenton and Corbeil and gave the Parisians a lot of trouble. Although he could no longer stop supplies reaching the city he managed to make it anything but easy. His troops were able to stop some of the convoys, and no one dared to venture beyond the city walls unless they were protected by a strong escort. The gate of St Denis was also occupied by royalist troops. The Leaguers succeeded in driving them out, but a few days later it was reoccupied by the King. He also made another attempt to enter Paris when some of his men presented themselves at the gate of St Honore disguised as peasants and carrying sacks of flour, but the trick was unsuccessful.

On 9th February 1591 the King surrounded Chartres, a town of considerable importance to the Parisians for it was one of the capital's granaries and vital to its existence. When the news reached Paris the excitement was intense, and the churches were filled with its inhabitants praying for divine assistance for the besieged town and raining down curses on the head of their king, whom they called a dog, a heretic, an atheist, a tyrant and many other unprintable names.

On 19th April, however, no 'divine assistance' having been forthcoming, Chartres opened its gates to the King, and the capture of Château-Thierry by Mayenne a few days later was a poor compensation for the loss of Chartres. During the summer months the King's generals, Montpensier and Biron, once again obtained control of most of the important towns in Normandy.

While this campaign was going on the King was reorganizing his army and by the autumn had an army of about 30,000 regular soldiers. The German contingent numbered 14,000, and Queen Elizabeth of England had reinforced the King's rmy with 6,000 English soldiers. In addition to these, 5,000 'gentlemen' voluntered to join and were gladly accepted. This came as a welcome surprise to the King, for after the siege of Paris had been called off many of his supporters who belonged to the '*noblesse de province*'* had returned disgruntled to their country seats. Henry IV therefore called the new volunteers his '*noblesse raffraichie*'.†

During the campaign in Normandy the King had hoped to capture Rouen, which for the last two or three years had been the only important Norman town which had permanently remained under the control of The League. It should not have presented any great difficulty as the town had no reserves of food or ammunition and its fortifications were in poor shape. Furthermore the governor of the town, Monsieur de Tavannes, did not get on well with the local authorities or the inhabitants. It was not until the month of December however, that the King's army appeared before the city gates, and by then the garrison had had plenty of time in which to strengthen its defences.

* Provincial nobility.
† Revived nobility.

The person responsible for this delay was Gabrielle d'Estrées, who had just succeeded Corisande as Henry's mistress. Ever since the summer of 1589, when the King was fighting in Normandy and never went back to Pau, Corisande had realized that their separation was inevitable and could not be far away. Although he frequently wrote to her, giving the latest news and protesting his undying love, she knew her Henry. It was most improbable that he could be away from her for so long and remain faithful. Someone else would soon turn up, and then it would all be over. It was not a case of 'absence makes the heart grow fonder', but 'out of sight out of mind'.

Corisande was quite right, for in the spring of 1590 the King had developed a passion for the Marquise de Guercheville, Antoinette de Pons. Much to his surprise and disappointment, however, it was unrequited. They first met in the spring of 1590, shortly after the battle of Ivry, when the King arrived late one afternoon at the Château de la Roche-sur-Guyon and asked if he could stay the night there. Antoinette, who had been a noted beauty at the French court during the reign of Henry III, said that she would be pleased to have him as a guest and made the necessary arrangements for accomodation for the King and his escort. She was, however, as virtuous as she was lovely, and, knowing her visitor's penchant for the ladies, she was not taking any risk and left the château just before dark to spend the night with friends in the neighbourhood.

Although the King had never previously received such treatment, he was quite unabashed, and during the siege of Paris wrote several letters to Antoinette, in one of which he even made a proposal of marriage which she ignored. Four years later the Marquise remarried and became the Comtesse de Liancourt, but Henry never forgot her, and after he married Marie de Medici he pursuaded her to appoint the Comtesse as one of her ladies-in-waiting. The Queen agreed, and on the occasion of the Comtesse's first appearance at Court, so the story goes, the King introduced her as one of the few women whose virtue had resisted his amorous advances.

It was in the same year in which he stayed the night in the Château de Roche-Guyin that he met Gabrielle d'Estrées, but it was not until the siege of Chartres in April 1591 that she became his mistress. After Chartres had surrendered, instead of

marching straight to Rouen, which was his next and most
important objective, he spent nearly three months with her at
the Château de Coeuvres, where she lived with her younger
sister Diane, after which he returned to Mantes and then,
despite the protests of Queen Elizabeth, who had sent substantial reinforcements for his army and wanted him to attack
Rouen as soon as possible, he proceeded to lay siege to Noyon.
This he did at Gabrielle's request and promised when the
town was captured to appoint her father Antoine d'Estrées as
governor. It was not until 17th August, however, that Noyon
was occupied and Gabrielle and her father installed there. The
English Ambassador sent a letter to Elizabeth explaining the
reason for this delay. "The King has chosen this town," he
wrote, "because of the great love he has for the governor's
daughter who has complete power over him." It was not until
the first week in December 1591, therefore, that the King and
his army commenced the siege of Rouen the plans for which
had been in existence since the beginning of the year.

Meanwhile Monsieur de Tavannes had been dismissed from
the post of governor because The League did not trust him, and
Villars-Brancas, from Provence, had been appointed to
succeed him.

The garrison had been reinforced and the fortifications
strengthened. When the siege opened the King called on the
city to surrender but received the reply that they were all
resolved to die rather than accept a heretic as the king of
France. Although the governor was not a bigoted Catholic he
realized that by fanning the flames of religious fanaticism he
could prolong the defence of the city, which might give
Mayenne or the Duke of Parma an opportunity to come to its
relief; and the usual anti-Huguenot demonstrations were
organized with the help of The Leaguers. The entire population
paraded in the streets headed by a troop of 300 barefooted
bourgeois, each of whom carried a large white candle. Behind
them marched 1,500 children dressed in white, and High Mass
was sung in the church of St. Ouen. The besieging army was
commanded by Maréchal Biron, as the King had marched
eastwards to ward off an attack by the Duke of Parma, who was
on his way to relieve the city. The siege continued until 24th
February 1592, and for ten weeks the battle raged to and fro.

On the final day at 7 a.m. three infantry regiments and several squadrons of cavalry made a sortie from the citadel and advanced on the trenches manned by Biron's troops and took them. Two hours later the battle was over and the defending garrison were masters of the situation. The attacking troops retreated in disorder, leaving 500 dead behind them.

When the Duke of Parma and Mayenne heard about the successful sortie of 24th February they thought that Rouen was safe and withdrew their forces behind the Somme. The King, having failed to come to grips with Parma, returned from Rouen and sent his own troops to reorganize themselves in the neighbouring provinces.

The Duke of Parma, now that the threat against Rouen no longer existed, withdrew and made for the town of Caudebec, which is situated on the right bank of the Seine about thirty miles from Rouen as the crow flies. It was held by the royalists, and his intention was to occupy it so as to ensure the free passage of ships trying to get to Rouen from the English Channel. He succeeded in doing so on 25th April, but during the course of the siege was severely wounded and decided to return to the Low Countries.

By this time the King had reinforced his army, and Longueville and Montpensier had also joined forces with him. They marched to the north of Caudebec to try and cut off Parma's retreat and force him to fight. Several skirmishes took place between the advance guards of the two armies near Yvetot, north of Caudebec, where the Spanish army had its headquarters. The Duc de Parma was now in a cleft stick for he could neither retreat nor advance. The English Channel was behind him, the Seine on his right flank and the King's army on his left barring the road to the Low Countries. His wound was so severe that he could no longer mount his charger. But he was an able and experienced general and did not lose his head. He succeeded in crossing the Seine at Caudebec in a fleet of small boats sent in haste from Rouen, marched along the left bank until he reached Charenton, where he re-crossed it. The road to Flanders was now open to him. He had saved his army, but a few months later he died of his wounds.

The King's fortune was now at its lowest ebb, and for some time there was little he could do. The royalists, however, had a few minor successes, including the capture of Epernay, which was of little or no importance save the fact that during the siege Maréchal Biron was decapitated by a cannon ball. For some time Biron's loyalty to the King had been cooling off, not that it had ever been wholehearted, and his son had reproached him saying, "If I were the King I would cut off your head." A statement which subsequently proved very ironical, for ten years later he himself was beheaded for treason.

It was not only in the north-east of France that the royalists had met with reverses. In almost all the other provinces where fighting was still going on they had lost ground: in Languedoc and Guyenne, and also in Maine and Anjou, where the defeat of the Protestants at the battle of Craon had resulted in their losing control of almost all their strongholds in both provinces. In May the Prince de Condé who was the King's Lieutenant-General in Maine, Anjou and Touraine had decided, in conjunction with the Prince de Dombes, governor of Brittany, to unite their forces and attack the town of Craon from which the Leaguer's garrison had been ravaging the whole countryside and cutting all lines of communications. Together their two armies numbered about 7,000 infantry and 800 cavalry, but they met with obstinate resistance, and before they could capture the town it was reinforced by Mercoeur, who arrived on the scene in the nick of time with 300 Spaniards. The royalist troops were attacked, and, although they suffered very few casualties, they withdrew.

By 1593 many people, even among the King's supporters, were beginning to wonder whether a Huguenot could ever succeed in imposing himself on a Catholic country. Henry himself began to have some doubts, but he would never admit complete defeat and was determined to fight although no one was more sorry than he was to see his kingdom so divided.

He tried to win Mayenne, the head of The League, over to his side, but he soon found that the question of religion was still the main bone of contention. Mayenne would not come to terms with the King unless he agreed to be converted to the Catholic faith. This Henry found difficult to do, for he wanted to be recognized as King before becoming a Catholic, for to do otherwise could be tantamount to admitting that heredity was not the legal basis of rightful succession to the throne in accordance with the accepted constitution. In order to overcome this, Villeroy, who was acting as go-between in the negotiations, tried to persuade the King to fix a date in advance when he would be prepared to abjure the Protestant faith and return to the Catholic Church. This became known as 'The Expedient', but it did not appeal to Mayenne, who feared that if he were to agree to it he might be left in the lurch by The League, which was still very powerful. But there was also another reason. Before he recognized Henry as the rightful King of France he wanted to be sure that the King would keep his part of the bargain, as he did not trust him. Mayenne's conditions were as follows. The King must be prepared to sign a treaty prohibiting the maintenance of royalist garrisons in all the towns in France and at the same time allowing The League to retain its own strongholds. Furthermore he insisted that he should be made the hereditary governor of Burgundy and be given the right of making all the ecclesiastical and governmental appointments within the province. The King considered that the situation was still not so hopeless that he should be forced to sign a treaty that amounted, in fact, to 'unconditional surrender', and he was not prepared, in any event, to accept Mayenne's final condition, which was that the treaty must be ratified by the Pope and Philip II of Spain.

As a last resort, therefore, the King decided in October to make overtures to Pope Clement VIII, who had succeeded Sixtus V, and the Cardinal de Gondi, who had taken part in the negotiations which Billeroy had conducted on behalf of Mayenne, agreed to approach His Holiness. The Pope did not share Mayenne's opinion and told the cardinal that the will of God was limitless, and if he wished he could recognize the King of Navarre as King of France whether he was a Catholic or a Protestant and, he continued, "As God's Vicar I would sooner die than dispute God's decision."

This impasse not unnaturally led to a hotbed of intrigue. The 'Cardinal *Roi*', as the Cardinal de Bourbon was called, had died. Charles de Vendome, who had succeeded him, and the Comte de Soissons, who wanted to marry Catherine de Bourbon, Henry's sister, both became pretenders to the throne. The King was determined to prevent this marriage and when he heard that Soissons had left for Pau to ask Catherine to

marry him, Henry wrote to Monsieur de Ravignan, who was
president of the Council of Béarn, "I have just heard the news,
with great displeasure that the Comte de Soissons has gone to
Pau to see my sister with a view to marrying her. All I want to
say to you is this that if you agree to this without my consent
you will answer for it with your head." Nevertheless, the very
fact that there were now two Catholic pretenders to the throne
was a great embarrassment to the King, for it might well
deprive him of the support of many of the Catholic royalists on
whom so much depended. Some of them were beginning to
think that he was being unnecessarily obstinate, and they considered whether they should not ask the King of Spain to issue
him with an ultimatum to abjure the Protestant faith or face
the consequences.

It was not only amongst the royalists that there were dis-
cordant views. There was also disatisfaction within The
League. Mayenne was regarded with suspicion, for 'Les
Seize'* were not sure that if it suited him he might not compromise with the King.

As 1592 came to an end the King took stock of the position.
What cards did he still have to play? The last two years had
been disastrous. His armies had suffered defeat after defeat and
had been severely depleted. The Swiss and the Germans had
returned home and the noblesse† had gone back to their
'châteaux and manoirs'. Henry had one trump card left in his
hand – abjuration, but how much longer could he wait before
playing it?

It was not an easy question to answer, and he had not done
so when the States General of Paris met on 26th January 1593,
having been convoked by the Duc de Mayenne. It was their
first sitting since 1588, when they met at Blois on the same day
as the assassination of Henri de Guise. Mayenne had previously
been against the idea of calling the States General together. As
head of The League he believed he could take the place of the
King, but until the death of the Duke of Parma he was not a
freelance as he was more or less under Spanish guardianship,
for The League had been relying almost entirely on Philip II
who held it in his hand. Without his help the Catholics would

* See footnote on page 96.
† See footnote on page 102.

not have been able to keep the King of France from sitting on his throne. The opening speech to the deputies of the States General, which was always given by the Sovereign at the opening of a session, was, on this occasion, made by the Duc de Mayenne. He gave a report of The League's work since 1588 and called on the assembly to advise what its future policy would be. He also assured them that he was ready to give his life to preserve the Catholic religion and maintain the constitution. It was apparent from the commencement of the session that the States General were divided into two opposite groups, one of which supported Mayenne and the other the King of Spain. The latter first proposed a resolution that the Infanta of Spain,* Isabella, should be elected Queen of France, but this raised such an uproar that its proposers withdrew the resolution and substituted another to the effect that either the young Duc de Guise or the Cardinal's nephew should be appointed. The Duc de Guise was Mayenne's nephew, so the deputies who supported the candidature of the Cardinal's nephew offered Mayenne, as compensation, the appointment of Lieutenant-General of the Kingdom, the province of Burgundy and a large sum of money. The States General made it abundantly clear, however, that they would never agree to a foreigner sitting on the throne of France.

Meanwhile a large body of Catholic supporters of the King had proposed that The League should reopen negotiations with him and suggested that a conference should be held at Suresnes. The States General agreed to this for it was just what the people of Paris wanted. They did not want to have to suffer the privations of another siege. As it was the wish of the States General, The League accepted this proposal, and when its delegates left Paris for Suresnes† to take part in the conference they were seen off by a large crowd demanding "peace at any price".‡

In addition to the delegation representing The League, the States General elected twelve of its members and the royalists eight, including the Archbishop of Bourges and a Huguenot named de Thou.

* The King of Spain's eldest daughter.
† In 1593 Suresnes was only a few kilometres outside the walls of Paris. It is now one of its suburbs.
‡ *La Paix à n'importe quel prix.*

The first two or three sessions of the conference were spent trying to draw up the conditions for a truce, and hostilities were suspended for ten days. This helped the royalist cause considerably, for it gave the Parisians a foretaste of what peace would mean to them, and this increased their desire for it.

On 5th May the conference was ready to start serious discussions. The Archbishop of Bourges was the first to speak on behalf of the royalists and was followed by the Archbishop of Lyons for the Leaguers. They both deplored the appalling state that the country was in, and the Archbishop of Lyons agreed but went on to say that France wanted a king who was a Christian not only 'in name but in effect' and that to accept a heretic as their King was contrary to 'divine right', the canons and rites of the Church and the basic laws of the State itself. The Archbishop did not dispute the fact that Henry IV was the rightful heir to the throne but said that his right to succeed Henry III was nullified by the fact that he was an heretic. If he were willing to return to the Catholic faith no one could properly object to him as their king.

The royalists asked for adjournment of the conference for three days. On 17th May it reassembled and the Archbishop of Bourges announced that the King had decided to abjure the Protestant faith and become a Catholic. The delegates departed.

The news spread from one end of France to the other like wildfire, and was generally received with great relief. But, as the King wrote in a letter to Gabrielle, it was a 'dangerous leap" to take, for the Protestants all over Europe were shocked and angry, and no one more than the Queen of England, who wrote and told him so in no uncertain fashion. But the King had not made his decision without considerable reflection and had carefully weighed up the pros and cons. What influenced his decision more than anything else was that the Protestants in France were in a large minority and the Protestant faith was never likely to become the national religion. Moreover he was sure that as a Catholic King he would be in a position to allow the right of freedom of worship to all his subjects and, as he is supposed to have said, "Paris is worth a Mass."*

The people of Paris were overjoyed when they heard the

* That he ever said this has been disputed by some of his biographers, but there seems to be no sufficient reason to disbelieve it.

news, and during the next few days thousands of them went to
St Denis, where the King had his headquarters, to see the man
"whom neither the Spaniard, nor The League nor the Pope
had been able to defeat", and they marvelled at what they saw.
Henry was his usual simple cordial self and showed no rancour
towards the same people who for the last three years had done
nothing but curse him. And this was not just a façade. They
were now his loyal subjects and he was a King who had the
welfare of all his people at heart. As the crowds surged round
him his guards tried to keep them away, but he gave them
orders not to do so but let the people come as near to him as
they wished. "If they want to see their King," he said, "let
them do so."

One of them, according to a story that has been handed
down, asked someone in the crowd, "Is this the same King who
we were told wanted to suppress us?"

"Yes," was the reply, "and he is much better looking than
the one we had in Paris.* He has a much bigger nose."

While all this was going on the King had been having other
troubles of a private nature, with his sister and his mistress.

When Charles de Bourbon, the Duc de Soissons had gone to
Pau to make a formal proposal of marriage to the King's sister
he was arrested, on her brother's orders, in her presence, not
withstanding the fact that she was acting as Regent of Navarre
and Queen of the Béarn. He was kept in custody for nearly a
week, after which he was conducted to the frontier of the
principality and forbidden to re-enter.

Princess Catherine was most upset, to put it mildly, but she
preferred to believe that the arrest of the Duc de Soissons was
the work of the States General of the Béarn and the Council of
Pau rather than of her own brother. She wrote a most moving
letter to him demanding an apology for the insult which she had
suffered. Shortly afterwards the King and his sister arranged
to meet at Saumur. They had not seen each other for five years,
and she fell into his arms. She then saw to her surprise and
embarrassment that she and her brother were not alone. The
Duc de Montpensier was with him. She soon discovered the
reason for his being there. Henry had brought him to Saumur
so that he could ask for his sister's hand in marriage. She told

* Henry III, the last of the Valois.

her brother, however, that it was out of the question that she
should become engaged to Montpensier, because not only had
she given her heart to the Duc de Soissons but had actually
signed a marriage contract. On hearing this, the King was
furious, and even his sister's tears had no effect upon him. He
cursed her in language which he had picked up from his peasant
companions in Coarraze when he was still a young boy.

But he had been having other troubles as well. In September
1592 his beloved Gabrielle had married a Monsieur de Liancourt, but the marriage only lasted for three months, for by
December she had left her husband to come to live with the
King. By the middle of 1593 Henry discovered that she was
already having an affair with Roger de Bellegarde, his Master
of Horse, who had been responsible for introducing her to him;
and considering the fact that before she first met him there had
been numerous other lovers he should not have been surprised.
When he first heard of Gabrielle's intrigue he sent her the
following letter.

> You complain of my suspicions but are not offended by the
> infidelity and treachery of others. . . . You also say that you will
> keep the promises you made me recently. You should not say
> 'I will keep them' but 'I am keeping them'. Make up your
> mind, my mistress, to have but one servant. You owe me that
> much. You will be doing me a great injury if you imagine that
> anyone else in the world could give you as much love as I do.
> No one could be as faithful to you as I am. If I have committed
> some indiscretions it is you who should take the blame for you are
> responsible for them. I want to see you again so much that I
> would willingly live the last four years of my life all over again to
> be able to do so as soon as this letter, which I end by kissing your
> hands a million times, reaches you.

He left her in no doubt, however, that this must not happen
again, for his letter ended with these words: "I will not forgive
you a second time."

The announcement that the King had at last crossed the
Rubicon was a bitter blow to the Spaniards, who had to act
quickly before it was too late. They began by trying bribery
and corruption. They had already won over a large number of
the States General deputies by giving them large sums of money,
and they followed this up by promising the colonels and

captains of the Paris militia "a substantial reward for their
services," but these were unwilling to accept any money if it
meant that they would have to acknowledge that it had been
paid to them by the King of Spain. The Church was also
offered generous compensation for the losses which it had
suffered as a result of the religious wars, and the Dean of the
Chapter of Notre-Dame refused to accept it. But there were
many who were not so scrupulous. During the first six months of
1593 the Spanish Ambassador succeeded in distributing no
less than 24,000 écus to the clergy, the Commons* and the
nobility. It was well worth the money if it ensured their
obtaining a minority in the States General in favour of a
resolution calling for a repealing of the Salic Law under which
women could not succeed to the throne of France, for otherwise
the Infanta of Spain could not become Queen.

When the Spanish Ambassador was convinced that a sufficient number of the deputies had been bought he demanded
that Mayenne should refer the matter to a vote in the States
General, and he agreed to do so. The case for a repeal was put
to the assembly and the House adjourned. However, many of
the deputies, including some of those who had not hesitated to
take the money, were not prepared to accept the Infanta as
their Queen unconditionally, and they asked the Ambassador
whether the King of Spain would marry his daughter to a
French Prince, but no satisfactory reply was forthcoming.

When the debate was resumed the Procureur General objected to any interference with the Salic Law, and the States
General decided that the laws and customs of their country
forbade them to accept as King of France someone who was not
a Frenchman.

The representatives of the King of Spain, however, refused
to abandon their claim for the Infanta and made some minor
concessions, but they were of no avail. Even Mayenne was
beginning to weaken, and the Archbishop of Lyons told the
Spanish Ambassador that if the States General decided to elect
a Queen because they were still not sure of their King it would
be a breach of the Salic Law. The deputies refused point blank
to interfere with the Salic Law or the principle of heredity. The
Spaniards realized that there was nothing more they could do

* Le Tiers Etat.

H

for the time being and agreed to a general truce for a period of three months. The proclamation was signed at La Villette on 31 July, by which time Henry IV had already been a Catholic for six days.

The theologians who had been appointed to receive the formal abjuration of the King, after clearing up any doubts he might still entertain about the basic tenets of the Catholic faith, met at St Denis on 21st July while the States General was still in session. He was not prepared to admit that he was a heretic spontaneously and without argument, and he did not try to conceal the mental anguish through which he was going. Furthermore, he refused to accept the procedure of abjuration which they proposed and insisted on making certain amendments in the form of service. When they finally found themselves in agreement, after several hours had been spent discussing the details, arrangements were made for the ceremony to take place in the old basilica of St Denis on Sunday 25th July.

The basilica was adorned with magnificent tapestries, and the streets leading up to it were strewn with flowers. At the head of the procession marched the Swiss with their drum-and-fife band, the mayor and his councillors and the French and Scottish guards. As the King advanced towards the west door of the church he was greeted by a fanfare of trumpets. He was dressed in a white satin doublet, a black cloak and a black hat with a plume of the same colour. White was the colour of the House of Bourbon, but the black cloak and hat which he had insisted on wearing were supposed to indicate that the heroic days of his life were over.

The Parisians were there in their thousands and greeted him with shouts of "*Vive le Roi*".

The Archbishop of Bourges, waited for him at the west door, and when the King approached asked him who he was.

"I am the King," Henry replied.

"What is it you want?"

"I beg leave to be received into the bosom of the Roman, Catholic and Apostolic Church."

"Is that your wish?"

"It is my wish and my desire."

The King then knelt down in front of the Archbishop and swore to live and die in the Catholic faith and to renounce all heresies which he formally condemned. The Archbishop then held out his hands so that the King could kiss his ring, pronounced the absolution and led His Majesty up the aisle to the altar where he confessed and took communion.

That evening, after a sumptuous banquet given in his honour at the palace of the Abbé* de St Denis, the King mounted his favourite charger and galloped to the top of Montmartre to look down below at the city that had been well worth a Mass. Below him the streets were crowded to the brim with the people of Paris and the sky was illuminated by the flames of many bonfires which had been lit to celebrate the occasion. The Parisians were, almost to a man delirious with joy, and for one night at least The League was forgotten.

However, in some of the provinces, where the Huguenots were more numerous there were no celebrations. Many of them felt that they had been betrayed by their leader and said that after the ceremony he had gone to bathe in the Seine to wash away the sin he had committed by attending Mass.

* Abbot.

8 The tide begins to turn

SHORTLY after the ceremony of abjuration when the States General reassembled at the Louvre for the purpose of prolonging the truce, which they only did under pressure of public opinion, they had still not recognized Henry as King, despite the fact that he had become a Catholic. They were still divided into two groups, both of which remained to some extent under the influence of The League, yet they would not go so far as to agree with Mayenne, who had adopted the pontifical attitude that the Bishops who had been appointed to prepare the King for his conversion had no authority to cancel the excommunication which had been pronounced by Pope Sixtus V, and that Henry still remained in the eyes of the Church, if not in those of his subjects, a heretic.

Nevertheless, although as a legislative body they did not formally acknowledge him as the rightful King of France, a large majority of them already did so in their heart of hearts and, after the assembly had adjourned on 8th August, did what they could in the provinces which they represented to bring the people round to their point of view. As a result of this The League lost control of many of the cities and towns which it had previously held. During the winter of 1593–4 Meaux, Cambrai, Fécamp, Aix-en-Provence, Peronne, Montdidier, Orleans, Bourges and Lyons either opened their gates to the King or surrendered after only a nominal resistance.

Realizing that the tide was turning in his favour, Henry tried to get the Pope to ratify his abjuration, and eventually, on 18th September, 1595, two years later, after a long diplomatic struggle, His Holiness deigned to recognize him as the 'Christian King of France'.

While these negotiations were going on, however, Henry was

preparing for the worst and reorganizing his army, which, by the date on which the truce was due to end, 31st December 1593, was strong enough to enable him, should it become necessary, to begin a complete blockade of Paris. But for the time being he decided to adopt a policy of 'wait and see'.

On 27th February 1594 the coronation of Henry IV took place in the cathedral of Chartres. Normally the Kings of France were crowned in Rheims, but it was still held by The League, and the governor Monsieur Saint-Paul refused to hand over the city, although he was urged by the inhabitants to do so. They were proud of their tradition and had no time for the intransigence of The League. The King hoped that his receiving the holy unction would put an end to the antagonism of the Catholic clergy.

Ever since the fifth century the oil used for this ceremony had been poured from the 'holy phial'* which St Remy had used at the baptism of Clovis, the first King of France, when he was converted from paganism and became a Catholic. It was, however, kept in Rheims cathedral and could not be made available, so a substitute had to be found. Fortunately, the Bishop of Chartres found another sacred vase at the abbey of Noirmoutiers, near Tours, the oil from which was supposed to have miraculously saved St Martin's life and which had since been kept at the monastery as a relic.

Eventually all the arrangements were completed for the coronation, but in the meantime the fact that it was to take place at Chartres was used as propaganda against the King by The League and some of the more bigotted Catholics, who lost no time in proclaiming that a coronation that was not solemnized in Rheims would be null and void.

The ceremony was performed by the Bishop of Chartres, assisted by five other prelates, and the King was anointed in the usual way. He took the oath and swore to protect the Church and clergy and guarantee their rights and privileges, and promised in the name of Jesus Christ to maintain peace between the Church and his people.

The King's coronation had repercussions throughout France but particularly in Paris, where it was exploited against The League. The people of Paris were tired of having a Spanish

* *La Sainte Ampoule.*

garrison in their midst and of the unceasing intrigues of The League against their King, whom they now almost revered. Mayenne decided that his position in Paris as head of The League was untenable, and exactly one week after the coronation he withdrew to the Aisne, where he thought it would be easier, as well as safer, to reorganize his scattered forces. As soon as he arrived there he sent an urgent appeal to the King of Spain for reinforcements.

With Mayenne temporarily out of the way, the time was ripe for Henry IV to enter his capital, but there were still difficulties in the way. The city was strongly defended, for, in addition to a large French garrison, the 4,000 Spaniards had not yet left and were already being re-equipped. It might, therefore, be difficult if not impossible to subdue the city without a fight, and the one thing the King was anxious to avoid was spilling French blood, yet at the same time he felt reasonably certain that most of the Parisians wanted him there.

By 21st March his army was ready, and he decided to take the risk. At 4 a.m. on the following day his troops arrived at the Porte Neuve*. They were met by Brissac, who had taken over command from Mayenne, and by the Provost of the city, Monsieur Lhuiller. Brissac had been secretly in touch with Mayenne since 6th March and had suggested that Mayenne's army as soon as it had been reinforced from Spain should advance and occupy the city, but as the reinforcements had not yet arrived Brissac had no alternative but to allow the royalist troops to enter. Marching along the bank of the Seine, they quickly reached the centre of the city, and the only resistance they encountered was from about twenty German soldiers, all of whom were either killed or thrown into the river.

About two hours later the King himself arrived at the Porte Neuve, dressed in full armour and accompanied by his archers and a mounted escort of about 400. He was met by Brissac and the Provost who handed over the keys of the city.

From there he went straight to Notre-Dame where he gave thanks to God and a Te Deum was sung. The bells of the cathedral rang out, and The Leaguers then knew that the King had entered the capital. After the thanksgiving was over the King left Notre Dame and rode through the streets of Paris.

* One of the city gates.

The people rushed out of their houses as he approached and greeted him with enthusiasm. The foreign troops who formed part of the garrison remained in their barracks and never stirred a finger, and the King told them that their lives would be spared if they withdrew. The same afternoon they marched away watched from the window of a house near the gate of St Denis by the King. Neapolitans, Walloons* and Spaniards. With them marched the King of Spain's representatives, Tascis, Ibarra and Feria – who was acting as the Spanish Ambassador. As they saluted the King, he called out to them, "Recommend me to your master but never come back." Henry was as surprised as he was overjoyed and so were the royalist troops, who could hardly believe their eyes.

He was as magnanimous in victory as he was defiant in defeat. When he entered the city he was determined to be merciful. He told the papal legate that as a representative of His Holiness he would have complete protection, and he sent a message to the Duchesse de Nemours, who was Mayenne's sister and to the Duchesse de Montpensier who was generally thought to have incited Jacques Clement to assassinate Henry III that he would call on them next day. He also granted an amnesty to most of the members of The League with the exception of a few whom he had less reason to trust than others, and they were outlawed.

No Leaguer was sentenced to death and not one was imprisoned – to the profound disgust of some of the more extreme Huguenots, who remembered their sufferings of the past twenty years. They would have liked to see all the leading members of The League either beheaded or thrown into the Bastille and said so. The King quickly put them in their places. "If those of you who think like that said the Lord's Prayer every day with a humble heart you would not say such things. I know that all my victories are given me by God's hand and he forgives me my trespasses as I forgive them who trespass against me."

Before he finally retired for the night overwhelmed by the day's events he received the members of the City Council who had come to do homage to him and confirmed them in their functions, although many of them had been his greatest enemies,

* Soldiers from the Low Countries.

and he also received in audience a delegation of Catholic clergy.

When they had all gone and he was left in peace and quiet with his Chancellor, Cheverny, he could still scarcely believe that it had all really happened.

"Mr Chancellor," he said, "Do you think that I am really here?"

"Sire," he replied, "you can be sure of it."

"I don't know," said the King, "for the more I think about it the more astonished I am. It is an act of God – one of his greatest."

9 Halfway home

EIGHTEEN years had passed since the King of Navarre, as he then was, left the Louvre in 1576, and even after his accession to the throne it had taken him five long years to return to Paris. A big step had been taken along the road to the pacification of the whole of his kingdom, but there was still a great deal to be done.

Nevertheless, his triumphal entry into the capital and the clemency which he had shown to those who had done everything in their power to prevent him returning had already won many of his subjects over to his side, particularly in the north. Before March was out, Rouen – the principal League stronghold in Normandy – Le Havre, Verneuil and Pont-Audemer had ceded to the royalists, and practically the whole of Normandy was under the King's control. A month later many towns in Picardy also deserted the League and by May Henry also had the upper hand in the greater part of Burgundy; and the contagion spread.

Now that Henry had returned to the Catholic faith and the question of religion was no longer important, the dislike of being occupied by foreign troops was beginning to have its effect on the people of France, who now suspected that the real reason why the King of Spain was supporting The League was that he hoped that by so doing he would divide the country into two camps. King Philip II had been extremely useful while it was necessary to rely on him for financial help and reinforcements, but now that Henry appeared to be firmly in the saddle the position had changed.

Even the young Duc de Guise deserted his uncle, the Duc de Mayenne, and handed over the city of Rheims after killing its governor Saint-Paul* with his own hand in the square outside

* See page 117.

Rheims cathedral. He soon became as close a friend of Henry IV as his father had been his rival and his enemy.

When he went to the Louvre to make his peace with the King he was not sure what kind of reception he would get. Henry, however, received him cordially and welcomed him to court, saying that he would get far more consideration from his sovereign than he had ever had from 'the other side'.

Guise was quite taken aback and started to make a long speech protesting his loyalty and regretting the feud which had existed between their two families for so many years, but the King interrupted after about two minutes and said,

> My cousin you are no better an orator than I am. I know what you want to say and it can be done in a very few words. We are all prone to the errors of youth. I will forget all the past and don't ever refer to it again. Know me for what I am and I will be a father to you, for there is no one at my court for whom I have greater regard than you.

The submission of so many towns and their governors to the King was not, however, made without some reserve, and it would be wrong to assume that it was done as an act of contrition. They did not regret having fought against the King while he remained a heretic, and it was only because at last he had seen the error of his ways that they ceased to be rebels. Many of them acted purely for selfish reasons and demanded, as the price of their loyalty, royal favours, perquisites and financial rewards; and some of them got what they wanted.

Villars-Brancas, for example, was appointed Admiral of France and received 715,000 écus; Paris cost the King 482,000 écus and several other towns and cities were rewarded with quite substantial sums of money.

Nevertheless, the King's decision to abjure the Protestant faith had already paid a handsome dividend, no matter how great the financial cost. In less than a year he had recovered at least half his kingdom which had previously been in the hands of The League.

Meanwhile the negotiations with the Pope to lift the King's excommunication were still continuing. They had been opened by the Controller of the Household, Brochard de la Clielle, who had been sent as an envoy to Rome by the Duc de Nemours to inform him officially of the King's conversion. A few days later Nemours himself arrived at the Vatican.

Clement VIII was in a difficult position for he did not want, for obvious reasons, to offend the King of Spain. Moreover he was not convinced that Henry's conversion was genuine, and was annoyed that the Gallican Church had decided to accept the King's act of abjuration without first consulting the Pope. He therefore told Nemours that he neither could nor did he wish to accredit an ambassador of the King of France to the Vatican, and that the action of the Bishop of Chartres and the five prelates who assisted him at the ceremony in Chartres cathedral was a palpable attack on papal supremacy. Nemours begged him in the name of peace to change his mind, but His Holiness refused. About a month after the Duc de Nemours had his unsuccessful first meeting with Clement VIII 'Les Seize' also sent a delegation to the Vatican. After the rebuff they had received since the King's entry into Paris – and they were expecting further defections in other parts of the country – they decided that it was high time that they tried to come to terms with him in order to protect their own interests and those of their followers. The delegation asked the Pope to intercede on their behalf, and he informed the King that they might be able to come to a satisfactory arrangement if he was prepared to release his subjects from their oath of fealty in the event of his changing his mind once again and leaving the Catholic Church. Any such undertaking would have to be ratified by His Holiness and the King of Spain.

Henry was only too willing to continue the negotiations, but he refused to allow the King of a foreign country to meddle in the internal affairs of France, and he insisted that the Pope had no authority to decide whether or not he was the rightful King. Provided the Pope was willing to agree to these two conditions, Henry was prepared to re-open the negotiations. He therefore sent the Abbé d'Ossat to Rome to find out whether the Pope was willing to accept them as a basis for negotiations and he succeeded in persuading His Holiness to give way on these two points. This was welcome news, but when the King was about to re-open negotiations with the Pope the position was suddenly worsened by an attempt on his life made by a young Jesuit, Jean Chastel.

On 27th December 1594, returning from a tour of Picardy and Normandy Henry stopped to spend the night with Gabrielle d'Estrées, who had borne him a son six months previously. When he entered her room he found several courtiers waiting to receive him. Among them was a young man, who managed, without anyone noticing him, to approach the King, and tried to stab him with a knife which fortunately just missed Henry's throat and did no more than cut his upper lip. At that very moment Monsieur de Montigny was embracing the King, and he threw himself on the would-be assassin and overcame him. The man was Jean Chastel, 19 years of age, the son of a Paris clothier, who had just left a Jesuit college at Clermont. The Court of Parlement* was ordered to try him for attempted murder.

When under cross-examination by the Procureur General, Chastel insisted that he had no accomplices and had himself planned to assassinate the King. Nevertheless he admitted that one of his tutors at the college, told him that if he did a good deed he would obtain a substantial remission of the period he would otherwise have to spend in purgatory, and he considered that he could do nothing which was more likely to gain him a remission than the assassination of a heretic. When asked who had told him this he said that it was Father Gueret, who had been his tutor for two and a half years. He had also been told that to kill the King would not be criminal because he had been excommunicated and Chastel was under no obligation to recognize Henry as the lawful King of France until the Pope had approved his accession to the throne.

The Court of Parlement then adjourned to the college of Clermont, where they found amongst the papers of one of the teaching staff, Father Guignard†, a document in which he had referred to Henry IV as 'the fox of Béarn' and regretted that he had not been 'despatched' during the massacre of St Bartholomew as had the other Huguenots. Guignard also 'glorified' Chastel's attempt to assassinate the King.

* At the end of the sixteenth century there were Parlements in seven of the French provinces as well as in Paris. They did not, however, have any legislative power, although they could make proposals regarding the royal edicts or object to them.

† Not Gueret.

This document corroborated the statement which had been made by the accused to such an extent that the Court of Parlement convicted both the professor and his pupil of attempted regicide and sentenced them to death. Chastel was 'quartered' by being tied by the arms and legs to four horses, and Father Guignard was hanged. The priests and scholars of the college of Clermont, and all other members of the Society of Jesus*, were 'banned from Paris and the Kingdom as corrupters of the young, disturbers of the public peace and enemies of the King and the State'.

The banishments of the Jesuits from France caused a sensation in Rome, and the Abbé d'Ossat feared for a time that it would mean the end of all negotiations with the Pope; but he was proved wrong, for Clement VIII decided otherwise, in spite of protestations from the Spanish Ambassador accredited to the Vatican. He organized a procession in which he took part barefooted and prayed for divine guidance, and on 30th August 1595 he announced at a Consistory Court that, subject to certain conditions, he would give the King absolution. The conditions were that Henry should admit that the absolution pronounced at St Denis was null and void, that he would proclaim the Council of Trent, re-establish Catholicism in the Béarn, and give preference to Catholics when making appointment to public offices. The Pope knew very well, as did the King himself, that some of these conditions could not be implemented in the near future, but as long as the King was prepared to accept them Clement was satisfied, for at least it would save his face. He refused, however, to pronounce absolution in advance. After referring the new conditions to the King, his envoys received instructions to accept them on his behalf.

On 17th September 1595, therefore, the ceremony of absolution took place in Rome in the absence of the King himself, who was represented by two of his '*Procureurs du Roi*'. The Pope was on his throne, and the King's representatives knelt down before him. They renounced the absolution of St Denis and asked the Pope, as the only person authorized, to give their King his absolution which he did by touching them on both shoulders with the papal staff.

* The Jesuits.

The announcement of the ceremony was, by order of the King, posted on the door of every church in France. The League had suffered a severe set-back.

While the negotiations had been going on in Rome the King's fight for peace had taken a new turn. Henry, now master of Paris and the greater part of his kingdom, had proclaimed in the Declaration of 17th January 1595 that he intended from now on to 'fight the King of Spain, on land and sea, and to avenge the wrongs and injuries which he had received'. His armies immediately resumed the offensive.

France had been invaded from five directions, but Burgundy was in the greatest danger. Biron, the son of Maréchal Biron who had been killed during the siege of Epernay, was in command of the troops there, and he had succeeded in occupying most of the fortified towns in the province which had been held by Mayenne, without meeting with any serious resistance except at Beaune, which only surrendered after a siege lasting three months. After Beaune had been captured, however, Biron was faced with a serious threat from the south-east by a large army of some 15,000 men under the command of Velasco, the Constable of Castille, who had crossed the Alps and had already reached the Franche-Comté and was marching on Burgundy. As Biron was outnumbered by the Spaniards by about three to one, he asked the King to come to his aid. Henry left Paris on 24th May 1595 and by 4th June had joined forces with Biron at Dijon, which had come over to the King's side but was now threatened by Mayenne.

Before he left Paris, however, the King ordered the Duc de Bouillon, one of his army commanders, to invade Luxembourg and occupy it and, at the same time, sent his troops from Lorraine to try and occupy the Franche-Comté which the Spaniards had just left. He hoped that in this way he could cut off their shortest line of retreat to the Low Countries and force them to make a long detour through Switzerland and Germany. When he had joined forces with Biron at Dijon the King decided not to wait for Velasco to attack the town and set off to meet the Spaniards with three regiments of cavalry, but when he reached Lux he detached a small force of cavalry from the main body of his army and marched towards Fontaine-Française, where he came in contact with an advance contingent of the Spaniards and found himself out-numbered by five to one. Faced with such overwhelming odds many a commander would have withdrawn his troops and 'lived to fight another day', but not Henry. He charged the Spaniards with such fury that they retired in disorder, and he was able to withdraw with the loss of only a few men and wait for Biron to arrive with reinforcements.

Meanwhile the Spaniards had been reinforced by Mayenne, who tried to persuade Valesco to send his infantry in to attack but, having suffered such heavy casualties at the King's hand, he refused and on the following day withdrew behind the river Saone and left Mayenne's Leaguers in the lurch. Mayenne was so disgusted with the Spaniards that he withdrew his own forces, ordered the garrison of Dijon to surrender the town, and from then onwards thought of nothing else but how he could make his peace with the King.

Henry had every reason to be delighted with the result of the skirmish at Fontaine-Française. As he wrote in a letter to his court at the Louvre telling them to celebrate the occasion, "200 of my cavalry prevented an army of 10,000 men entering the Kingdom".

With Valesco now out of the way the King was free to carry the war into territory held by the enemy, and within a few days he had subdued the Franche-Comté, and by the beginning of September he had occupied the whole of Burgundy and entered Lyons.

The King, in the moment of victory, magnanimously offered a truce to Mayenne, which he was only too glad to accept, though it did not please the King's ministers who protested to him about it. He told them, however, that "it is always dangerous to press a desperate man too far and above all a man of the quality of the Duc de Mayenne". Once again Henry IV had demonstrated, as one of his biographers wrote, that he had "the characteristics of both a fox and a lion."

Nevertheless everything had not been going so well in some of the other provinces. The King's army in Brittany had only made some slight progress, and Doullens in Picardy had been lost to the enemy, but the successful conclusion of the King's negotiations with the Pope regarding his excommunication had more than made up for these minor reverses. A week after

Clement VIII had lifted the excommunication by absolution
on 18th September the truce between the King and Mayenne
in Burgundy was extended to the whole of France, and Mayenne opened negotiations regarding his submission to the
King's authority. A treaty was signed at Fontainebleau on 24th
January 1596. In it Mayenne formally recognized Henry IV as
the rightful king of France, and received by way of compensation 3 million livres to enable him to pay the debts which he had
contracted during the war. Nor was this all. Joyeuse also signed
a treaty with the King, by which he received, in return for his
submission to the Crown, a Marshal's baton and the governor-
ship of the Languedoc.

Nevertheless, Mayenne had not had it all his own way. It is
true that he had been well paid for his newly-conceived loyalty
to his King, but according to a story told by Sully in his
Memoirs, Henry, whose sense of humour could be sardonic if he
chose, had managed to get a dig at his cousin during the first
meeting at the Château de Monceaux which led up to the
treaty of Folembray, Mayenne apart from being much too fat for
the good of his health also suffered badly from sciatica. One day,
during an interval in the morning's discussions, Henry took him
out into the garden to get a break of fresh air and walked so fast
that poor Mayenne could not keep up with him and soon started
puffing and lagged behind. Seeing this, Henry turned round,
slapped him on the back and said, "Tell me, my cousin, am I
going too fast for you?" When Mayenne said that he was and
asked for the King's indulgence, Henry quickly replied, "I
promise you in God's name that this is all the vengeance you
will get from me," and having said that took his panting
cousin back to the château, where he revived him with two
bottles of Arbois*.

This was not the only verbal sally which Mayenne had to
take from the King at Monceaux, for the French historian
l'Estoile has written of another occasion when Mayenne had
arrived at the Château and was greeted at the door by Henry
and his mistress, Gabrielle d'Estrées. When Henry saw who was
there, he welcomed him warmly and then said, "My cousin is
it really you I see or am I dreaming?"

* Arbois is a wine-growing district in the Department of the Jura, part
of the province of the Franche-Comté.

Gabrielle d'Estrées, the mistress of Henry IV, in her bath

Henry IV with Marie de Medici and his family

By this time the only real resistance to the King's authority
was in Brittany, where Mercoeur, who had received further
reinforcements from Philip of Spain, was still in control. The
Spaniards had already occupied the fortress of Crozon which
dominated Brest and the Rade,* but when it was surrounded
by the royalists under the command of Maréchal d'Aumont,
and the garrison commander appealed to Mercoeur to come to
his assistance, Mercoeur refused. Aumont then took Crozon and
massacred the whole of the Spanish garrison. Mercoeur's
refusal was, doubtless, due to the fact that, although he was
only too willing to use Spanish troops to fight against the King,
he realized that Philip's only interest in holding Crozon was
because he wanted control of Brest, which would have provided him with a most useful naval base on the sea route from
Spain to the Low Countries. Mercoeur did not recognize
Henry IV as the King of France, but he was, first and foremost,
a Frenchman.

Henry was not slow to appreciate that, with the gradual
breaking up of the anti-royalist forces due to the submission of
their commanders, the Spanish troops in France – who were
still large in number – might soon find themselves in serious
difficulties and decide to withdraw to the Low Countries. In
order to cut off their retreat, therefore, he laid siege to La Fère,
which is about 100 miles north-east of Paris and was then held
by the Spaniards. The town which was strongly fortified and
surrounded by marshlands was extremely difficult to approach.

The besieged garrison dammed the river Oise to form a large
reservoir and then opened the dam, hoping thereby to sub-
merge the whole town, leaving only the fortress standing. All
they succeeded in doing, however, was flooding the lower part
of the town, which forced the inhabitants to live for the next
few weeks in the upper storeys of their houses. The damming of
the river, therefore, came back on them like a boomerang. It
was now almost impossible either to leave or enter La Fère.
Supplies soon got so low that after a siege of six months the
beleagured garrison had to surrender.

Unfortunately the King does not appear to have realized the
importance of Calais to the Spaniards and obviously forgot that

---

* The Rade de Brest is a large bay almost completely surrounded by
land, lying between Brest itself and the Cap de la Chevre.

I

Philip had had his eyes on it for a long time because, for one thing, it was the nearest port to England on the French side of the English channel. Before the royalist troops which were stationed on the north-eastern frontier between France and the Low Countries got to hear of it, a Spanish force under the command of Rosne, a former Leaguer now in the service of Philip, marched on Calais and occupied the surrounding villages, and the new governor of the Low Countries, the Archduke Albert*, quickly crossed the border and joined forces with him. Calais was captured on 17th April, 1596.

Meanwhile the King was getting very short of money, and there were only 25,000 écus left in the Treasury. He sent an urgent letter to Sully who was the equivalent of his Chancellor of the Exchequer.

> Unless I can quickly get sufficient funds to meet the heavy expenses which have to be incurred, [he wrote] I shall soon be in great difficulty.
> My Swiss soldiers are deserting every day and my cavalry cannot carry on if they don't get paid. . . . We are also short of flour and the troops have only half the provisions they need and sometimes get nothing.

Even Henry himself was almost down to rock bottom for in another letter he wrote,

> I should like you to know the state in which I find myself, which is such that I cannot even get face to face with the enemy. I have hardly one charger on which I can ride into battle or a saddle to put on its back, my shirts are all in rags and my doublets worn at the elbow. My soup bowl is frequently empty and for the past two days I have dined and supped with friends who have apologized for having practically nothing to put on the table because for the last six months they have received no money.

The King was extremely worried, but not desperate, and shortly after the occupation of Calais by the Spaniards his luck turned. The Archduke Albert hurriedly withdrew his army over the Dutch border, where it was urgently required to reinforce the troops who had suffered severe casualties during the siege of Huist.

* Archduke Albert of Austria.

The fall of Calais had alarmed the Queen of England, who saw the occupation, as it clearly was, 'as a dagger pointed at the heart of England'. After the King's abjuration of the Protestant faith she wrote and gave him a piece of her mind, but, although she then began to have doubts about his reliability as an ally, she was well aware that in the war with Spain they had a common cause. In July 1596 she signed a treaty of alliance and promised to provide him with 4,000 men to carry out an operation on the high seas which would 'ruin the trade of Spain and destroy a large part of the Spanish fleet'.

This was excellent news, but steps still had to be taken to put the country's finances on a firmer footing. The King decided to make an appeal to the nation and called a conference of bishops, noblemen, magistrates and aldermen from all the provinces. This was held at Rouen to discuss and consider how sufficient funds could be raised "to raise an army strong enough to prevent the enemy from ravaging the whole of France and sacking every town at their pleasure."

When the conference met the King opened the proceedings with a fervent appeal for help. He told the delegates that he had called them together to advise him as to the ways and means of raising the money that was so urgently needed and succeeded in persuading them to vote for the imposition of a tax of one sol* in the pound on all goods sold. It had, nevertheless, taken all his powers of persuasion – and they were considerable – to convince the delegates that this was necessary. When he entered the big hall of the Abbey of St Ouen he met with a very cool reception. They considered that they were already over-taxed, and some of them did not relish having to pay more still to get involved in a war with Spain. However, his opening speech, which was a mixture of good sense and *bonhomie* swayed them round and greatly impressed them, for it was the first occasion since his accession to the throne that he had ever appeared before a national assembly. They could not help comparing him with the three useless monarchs who had preceded him and had ushered out the Valois dynasty with such incompetence. They realized for the first time that the throne of France was occupied by a king who was not only a great soldier but a statesman.

* Sou.

If I had wanted to acquire the reputation of being a great orator, [he told them] I would have prepared a long harangue and delivered it with grave solemnity. But I should like to be remembered as something quite different, as the liberator and saviour of the State. For what have I assembled you here? You know as well as I do that when God called me to the throne of France I found my kingdom not merely half ruined but almost completely lost. By the grace of God, and the profession of arms, by the swords of my brave noblemen and by my own endeavouring I have so far saved the country. Let us continue to do it now in its hour of trial. I have not called you together as my predecessors did, to give my consent to your wishes, but to receive your good advice and follow it, in other words to put myself under your guardianship, a wish not often entertained by grey-bearded and victorious Kings.

Gabrielle d'Estrées, who heard his speech from the back of the hall where she sat hidden behind a tapestry, afterwards congratulated him, but said that she was surprised to hear him say that he wished to put himself under their guardianship. "It is quite true," he replied, laughing, "but, Zounds*, I mean with a sword by my side."

Having now obtained the resources and reinforcements which he so badly needed, the King was planning an attack on Arras. He established his base for the operation at Amiens, where he accumulated a large store of ammunition and supplies, and intended to station Swiss troops there to defend it, but the inhabitants refused to have a garrison in the city. When the new of these preparations for an offensive reached the Spanish governor of Doullens he made a surprise attack on Amiens and captured it without much difficulty.

Meanwhile Henry had left Rouen and returned to Paris with Gabrielle d'Estrées, who was expecting another child†, and it was when the city was in the middle of the festivities of 'Mi-Careme'‡ that the news of the disaster arrived in the night. He said goodbye to his mistress, telling her that he must leave her as he had a new war on his hands, but she very soon followed him as she was frightened to remain in Paris without him. The King mounted his charger and set off for Picardy.

* By God's wounds,' the English equivalent of the French, *Ventre Saint-Gris*.

† The child (Catherine-Henriette) was born on 11th November 1596.
‡ Mid-Lent.

The capture of Amiens by the Spaniards was a bitter pill to swallow, for its occupation by the enemy had closed the river Somme and was a direct threat to Paris. Worried as he was, however, Henry refused to panic, although all the equipment, ammunition and supplies in the base of Amiens were now in the enemy's hands. He offered Calais to the Queen of England if she would double the number of the English contingent which she had agreed to let him have by the treaty signed at Greenwich in the previous year and promise to keep it 'as belonging to the Crown of France and as a pledge for money already lent and to be lent, until it has all been refunded'. He also raised more money by increasing the tax on salt by 15 sols a minot.†

After visiting a number of towns in Normandy to reassure them he sent Maréchal de Biron to lay seige to Amiens and station troops along the frontier between France and Flanders to prevent supplies and reinforcements reaching the city. The King was sure of one thing, however, namely that as Amiens was not strongly defended it could not withstand a long siege.

By 8th June the King had taken over command of the besieged army from Biron. He had a force of about 30,000 and a plentiful supply of ammunition. He succeeded in stopping an army under the command of the Archduke Albert of Austria from relieving the beleagured garrison, and on 18th September 1597 it surrendered.

It was evident after the fall of Amiens that peace was not far off. This victory had put an end to the Spanish offensive, and their army once more withdrew towards the Low Countries. This was fortunate for Henry, as his own army had to be disbanded immediately. All he was left with was 500 cavalry, so he could not exploit his success. Nor was the King of Spain in a better position to continue the fight. His fleet had been destroyed, and his armies were beaten. The English and the Dutch had plundered his colonies and were ravaging his sea-coast.

The Pope, who relied so much on the power of Spain, was worried and sent his nephew Cardinal Aldobrandini to persuade King Philip to sue for peace which he did. It had needed the recapture of Amiens and the expectation that he would

† 15 sous a peck (equivalent in dry weight to two gallons).

soon be dead to convince him that his ambition for world conquest was now a castle in the air.

On 28th January 1598 peace negotiations were opened at Vervins by the mediation of the Pope and resulted in a treaty being signed on 2nd May. When the negotiations started Henry IV wrote to Queen Elizabeth, "Our just arms assisted by the grace of God have at last humiliated our enemy for he has asked for peace and declares that he will go to any reasonable lengths to obtain it."

But Elizabeth was not at all pleased about the Treaty of Vervins. In 1596 Henry had promised that he would not conclude a separate peace with Philip and had offered to act as mediator between Spain and his two allies, England and Holland. He intended to include them both in the treaty, but as it appeared that they still had good reasons for carrying on the fight with Spain, whereas France had none, he did not want to jeopardize the chance of obtaining peace by refusing to sign a treaty with Philip unless England and Holland were included. All the Dutch wanted was to be given independence and liberty of conscience, but the English were quite happy to continue fighting on the high seas and capturing Spanish galleons loaded with gold and silver. Elizabeth thought that Henry had let both countries down and told him so, but Henry felt that he could not risk losing his throne and his kingdom for the sake of an ally whom he regarded as unreliable.

With the Treaty of Vervins the long struggle between France and Spain ended. France had been through a terrible time during the religious wars which had brought death and destruction in their wake. Out of a total population of about 14 million some 4 million had perished, and there was hardly a province in the whole of France which had not been ravaged and pillaged. In Picardy widows and orphans formed the greater part of the population. Nevertheless, France had got rid of the foreign troops, and that was something gained. She had also maintained her independence.

King Philip was bankrupt by the end of 1597 and had been forced to abandon all his grandiose plans. Spain had ceased to be a great power.

While the peace negotiations were still going on Henry IV had not been idle. With quite a small army he marched into

Brittany – the only province which had not yet submitted to his authority – but he did not have to fight. Mercoeur, as soon as he learned that the royalist army was approaching and knowing that he now stood alone, gave in but not until he had been promised, like Mayenne and the other leading Leaguers, generous terms and financial compensation. This he received and, in addition, his sister was promised the hand of Henry's eldest son by Gabrielle d'Estrées, although he was only four years old. He was already known as 'Monsieur', despite the fact that he was a bastard.

Having obtained control of Brittany the King then marched on Nantes, where he was welcomed by the municipal authorities and given the keys of the town. When they were handed over to him with great ceremony by the chief Magistrate he expressed his thanks but said that what would give him greater pleasure would be the keys of the hearts of the people of Nantes, thereby confirming once again his magnaminity to those who had for so long refused to recognize him as King. All he wished to do was to forget the past.

It was while he was still in Nantes, three weeks before the Treaty of Vervins was concluded and a week before Gabrielle d'Estrées bore him a second son, Alexandre, that the King signed the Edict of Nantes, which he declared to be 'permanent and irrevocable': the charter of the rights and privileges of the French Protestants.

They received, amongst other things, the right to hold ministerial and government appointments, which had previously been denied to them, the right of freedom of worship in all but five places which were specified in the edict, subject to their loyalty to the King, and the right to make wills which previously they had been unable to do. The Edict of Nantes also provided for the organization of the Protestant clergy into a synod, colleges and consistories, the creation in the Parliament of Paris of a 'Chamber of the Edict' and of a bipartite chamber in the Parliament of Toulouse.

The Edict did much to re-establish the King in the eyes of all the French Protestants, many of whom had been shocked and disillusioned when he abjured the Protestant faith at St Denis. It also showed, once and for all, that, having been "the victim as well as the hero of the religious wars", as he himself put it, he was determined to rebuild France on new foundations of which the corner stones were to be "tolerance and liberty". He had seen enough of what dissension and bigotry could do, and he intended to ensure that religious beliefs would be divorced from politics.

When the general terms of the Edict of Nantes became known there was, of course, much opposition from the Catholic clergy, and the Pope called it the most "abominable edict" that it was possible to imagine. The King wisely decided therefore, to make some concessions, one of which was that the Catholic religion would be re-established in the Protestant strongholds and that in all the towns which continued to be held by the Protestants the Catholic clergy would not have to contribute towards the payment of ministers salaries. He also agreed to limit the freedom of the synods which the Edict had allowed the Protestant clergy to form. Later in 1599, however, the King lifted these restrictions.

When the Edict was discussed in the Parlement of Paris there were more objections, and the King made further concessions, but they were only of a minor nature. The main thing was that the Edict of Nantes ushered in an era of tolerance between two Churches both of whom, while worshipping the same God and accepting the general principles of the Christian faith, hated each other. From henceforth they would both have to live in a state of peaceful co-existence even if they still had no respect for each other, and nowhere else in Europe during the sixteenth century was there a similar state of affairs.

It was too optimistic, however, to think that this could go on for ever. Although it was what Henry had always wanted it had only been brought about by the force of circumstances; the accession of a Protestant King to the throne of France and the fact that both sides, after many years of religious warfare, wanted some respite. The Edict was, therefore, more in the nature of an armistice than a permanent peace. Henry was as aware of this as anyone else and had made it clear in the preamble to the Edict, when he regretted that it was not "as yet God's wish" that He should be worshipped by all the Frenchmen "in the same form of religion". There was no doubt that the general feeling in the country at that time was that all its people should be of the same faith. The time was not yet ripe for religious tolerance to be regarded as a Christian virtue.

The Edict, however, was to last for eighty-seven years, for, although the rights and privileges during the previous twenty years had been gradually whittled down, it was not until 17th October 1685 – an ill-fated day for France – that Louis XIV signed the Revocation of the Edict of Nantes, whereby the Protestants were deprived of their right of publicly practising their religion. It was, perhaps, the greatest mistake Louis made during the whole of his reign, for France lost more than 400,000 of her most able inhabitants in the army, the navy, the judiciary and in commerce. As many members of the Reformed Church as were able to leave emigrated to England, Holland, Germany and America, where they set up Huguenot colonies.

10 Second wind

It was shortly after the signing of the Edict of Nantes that Henry IV said, "France and I have need to get our second wind." He was still only 40 years old, but the past twenty-five years of struggle and strife were beginning to leave their mark upon him, and he already looked much older than his age. His face was heavily wrinkled, his skin had become the colour of parchment, and his beard had turned quite white. The Venetian Ambassador said that he looked at least 60 and bore the signs of all the trials and tribulations which he had suffered. Nevertheless his physical appearance belied him, for his powers of resistance and vitality were as strong as ever. Moreover, he had gained by experience a knowledge and understanding of his people which was to stand him in good stead in the coming years in which so much still had to be done to put France on her feet again.

It was also at this moment that the King nearly made what would have been the greatest mistake of his life and might well have had disastrous repercussions.

Of all his mistresses, and they were many in number, Gabrielle d'Estrées was the one for whom he cared most. He really loved her deeply, and she had borne him three children. He intended to marry her in the spring of 1599 and have her crowned as Queen.

Ever since his triumphal entry into Paris in March 1594 Gabrielle had lived with Henry in Paris and had accompanied him on State visits to a number of places. She was by his side at all official functions and went hunting with him. She was, to all intents and purposes, a Queen without a crown, and she had given him much in return. Before she met Henry, however, she had had many lovers, and during the last six years she had openly had many more. Although the King knew of her affairs he had been extremely tolerant, and, with the exception of passing flirtations with Mademoiselle de Hauraucourt, Madame des Fosses and Mademoiselle Havard de Senante, one of Gabrielle's ladies-in-waiting, he himself had almost begun to turn over a new leaf.

However, he wanted to marry her not because of his love and affection but for reasons of State. The question of an heir to the throne had become of great importance and who was going to succeed him? Marguerite de Valois had borne him no children, but he already had two sons by Gabrielle, and she was again with child. The King had done so much during the past few years to save his kingdom from self-destruction, but if there was no legitimate heir to the throne when he died all this might be thrown away, and a foreigner might succeed him. He did not want the Bourbon dynasty to come to an end prematurely.

In 1598 the King had taken Sully into his confidence and spoke of the importance of having an heir to succeed him. There were only three qualities, he said, that his future wife must have: she must be beautiful, of a sweet disposition and be able to give him children. He searched all the Courts of Europe without success for someone with all these qualties and who was also eligible to be the Queen of France. It had been suggested to him that he should marry Marie de Medici, but this found no favour in his eyes, for not only was her family 'of recent origin' but she was related to Catherine de Medici, '*La Serpente*'. The King left no doubt in Sully's mind that Gabrielle d'Estrées possessed all the three qualities which he had already mentioned.

Sully listened to what the King had to say and then warned him of the dangerous situation in which he would find himself if he carried out his intention of marrying Gabrielle. The people did not mind her being his mistress, but many of them would not like the future King of France to have a mother who was generally regarded as a whore.

In any event there was another obstacle to the marriage. Marguerite de Valois was still the King's legal wife, although she had never been crowned as Queen. Ever since 1593 attempts had been made to persuade her to release him from his marriage, so far without success. Marguerite would not have minded losing him as a husband, but she was not prepared to do anything which would pave the way for a bastard son to become the rightful heir to the throne. On 7th February 1599, however, Marguerite quite unexpectedly changed her mind and wrote a charming letter to Gabrielle, in which she promised to take the necessary steps to have the marriage annulled by the Pope.

As soon as the King learned of this new development he immediately sent an Ambassador to Rome with a request that Clement VIII should act quickly, and he fixed the date of the wedding for the first Sunday after Easter.

What would have happened had fate not intervened will never be known, but before any reply had been received from the Vatican Gabrielle died. On 9th April she had given birth prematurely to a stillborn child, a son. Thirty-six hours later she died in agony, having lost first her speech, secondly her hearing and finally her sight, and after her death her face, which had always been so beautiful, shrivelled up and came a hideous mask. Her enemies, and she had many, said that it was the work of the Devil to whom she had sold herself to become the King's mistress.

The death of Gabrielle d'Estrées was so sudden and unexpected it was not surprising that many people thought that she had been poisoned. However, a Commission of Inquiry, appointed by the King to investigate the circumstances of her death, found no evidence to support any such suspicion. Some of Henry's advisers and greatest supporters attributed it to 'the hand of God' and rejoiced in the fact that it had saved France from 'a great peril'. One of them wrote to the Cardinal de Givry saying, "God has spoken to the King and the Kingdom clearly and intelligently". Even Sully, when expressing his sincere condolences for the King's bereavement, could not resist saying that he hoped His Majesty realized that providence had intervened in a just cause.

Nevertheless, there were some who remained convinced that Gabrielle's death was mysterious, a conviction which was confirmed by a story which came from Rome. When Henry IV's ambassador went to the Vatican to ask the Pope to annul his marriage to Marguerite, Clement, who, for obvious reasons, was not anxious to comply with the King's wishes wanted some time to think the matter over. According to the story His Holiness prayed every evening for divine guidance on this difficult problem. Eight days before Gabrielle's death, just as he had finished praying, he looked up towards heaven as though he had seen a vision, and said, "God has provided the answer". Whether the story is true or not there can be no doubt what the answer was.

For a short while Henry was inconsolable, and he wrote to his sister Catherine de Bourbon, telling her that never again would he love another woman. He went into mourning for three months, but before two of them had passed he became passionately in love with Mademoiselle Henriette d'Entragues, who was the most blatantly immoral and scheming of all his women. She was the daughter of Marie Touchet, who had been the mistress of Henry's brother-in-law Charles IX and had made his life a misery. Her father, François d'Entragues, had been a supporter of the House of Guise, but he was always willing to support anyone if he thought it would be to his advantage. She also had a sister, named Marie, who was a bigger strumpet than she was. There was hardly a family in the whole of France who had a worse reputation than the d'Entragues.

Henriette was only 20 years old when the King first met her in Blois only a couple of weeks before Gabrielle d'Estrées' confinement. Maurice Andrieux, in his life of Henry IV has described her as "a lovely brunette with intelligent and provocative eyes, a tall svelt figure and endowed to an extraordinary degree with what in modern language is known as 'sex-appeal'."

The King was completely taken in by her, and it was not long before he had forgotten that Gabrielle had ever existed. When he first tried to seduce her she told him that it would cost him a lot of money as her fee was 100,000 écus. She obviously either had a very good opinion of herself or knew that once Henry became intrigued by a good-looking woman he would stop at nothing in order to possess her. But even he was taken aback, for although he had bestowed titles and granted large allowances to some of his former mistresses, 100,000 écus was a lot of money and more than Sully, who controlled the Privy Purse, was prepared to pay without a vigorous protest. Nevertheless, the King got his own way, although he is supposed to have said when he saw several bags of écus on the table next morning that it was more than enough to pay for one night's enjoyment.

100,000 écus, however, was not all that Henriette wanted, for she had a greater ambition than to be merely the King's mistress; she wanted to be the Queen of France and she made it clear to him that she would not be his mistress. In addition to the generous subsidy, therefore, Henry created her the Marquise de Vernueil and signed a document in which he promised to make her his Queen provided that within a year she bore him a son. This ensured that he would continue to have access to her, but he had no intention of keeping his part of the bargain.

Meanwhile the King's advisers implored him to reconsider his previous decision not to marry Marie de Medici, but he refused to listen to them until the Parlement of Paris intervened. He was left in no doubt about what the Parlement thought of his liaison with Henriette d'Entragues, and he was told that it was essential in the interests of France and of the Crown that he should marry someone who was more suitable to be his Queen. In September 1599, therefore, he decided to reopen negotiations with the Holy See for the annulment of his marriage with Marguerite de Valois.

Henriette soon got to hear of this and reminded Henry of his promise and the fact that it was in writing and signed by him. In order to try and pacify her he suggested that she should entrust the document to a Capucin monk named Hilaire, whom she knew and trusted, with instructions that he should go at once to the Vatican and deliver it to the Pope, who would doubtless take suitable action to prevent the King's marriage to Marie de Medici. He was determined, however, that the document should never reach the Pope, and he arranged for the French Ambassador to the Vatican, the Cardinal d'Ossat to have Hilaire met at the gates of Rome and forced to hand over the document.

Henriette must have suspected that this was a trap, for she did not immediately hand over the document; but later she changed her mind and Hilaire arrived at the Vatican.

The Cardinal was ready for him and managed to persuade His Holiness that the document was of no value and that Hilaire should be unfrocked for having allowed himself to be involved.

On 17th December, therefore, after receiving a report made by a commission of three bishops whom the Pope had appointed to advise him before making a decision, the annulment was pronounced at the Vatican, and in the following spring the marriage contract was signed in Florence.

The King, however, had other problems on his hands. The first and foremost was to repair the ravages of the last forty years of religious warfare, and the second to prepare for another campaign. To find sufficient money for the latter was not going to be easy unless he was prepared to use part of the large dowry which Marie de Medici was going to bring with her. There was, in fact, not the slightest doubt that he would do this, and in any event Sully would have made him for Marie de Medici had been chosen because she was a member of the famous family of Florentine bankers. The sum agreed upon was 600,000 golden écus. Rosny, who, with another of the King's advisers, had gone to Florence to carry out the negotiations with the Grand Duke of Tuscany, Marie de Medici's father, had hoped to obtain a larger dowry, but as the matter was urgent he settled for 600,000. When he returned to Paris Sully brought him along to see the King. "Where have you been?", Henry asked him, to which Rosny replied, "We have just married you." The King was taken by surprise, for he had hoped that the negotiations would take much longer. He said nothing for about ten minutes but sat scratching his head and biting his nails.

Finally he clapped his hands and spoke. "Well, well," he said, "If God wishes it there is nothing to be done. If you say it is necessary for the good of my Kingdom and my people that I should get married – so be it." Nevertheless he told them that he sincerely hoped that his second marriage would be happier and less complicated than the first.

He insisted that the marriage should be postponed for some months, however, because of the war with the Duc de Savoie which was imminent and would keep him busy for the time being. This started the gossip at the King's court talking, for they had for some time been hinting that a member of the Italian bourgeoisie was hardly a suitable consort for the King of France. Henriette d'Entragues was not slow to join in the criticism and on one occasion impudently asked Henry when he was going to bring Marie de Medici to Paris, to which he quickly replied, "As soon as I have got rid of all the court whores."

The campaign which Henry IV was about to open in Savoie had as its objective the recapture of the Marquisat de Saluces, the hereditary property of the Dauphins of France* which the Duc de Savoie had appropriated in 1588 when the King of France, Henry III, was not in a strong enough position to oppose him. Henry had given him an ultimatum to the effect that if the Marquisat had not been handed back to France before the end of 1600 he would send an army to take it by force, but he decided at the end of June that he was not prepared to wait any longer. He therefore marched into Savoie at the head of his army early in June and by the end of the month had captured the town of Chambery and, by the beginning of September, two other important towns.

As the campaign appeared to be proceeding according to plan, the King wrote to his fiancée and asked her to leave for France as soon as possible. By 6th September he was able to write and tell her that with the exception of Bourg the whole of the province of Bresse was in his hands and that the Duc de Savoie should in future be known as the 'Duc *Sans* Savoie.†

For the next few weeks he continued to send the Princess‡ letters saying how much he loved her and how he was longing to meet her. There was, however, an unpleasant shock in store for him. He had no idea that she was very plain and physically unattractive, for when it had first been suggested that he should marry her he had been shown a portrait of her which was extremely flattering.

Philippe Erlanger has described her as having

> a majestic bearing, a pale complexion, large arms and an opulent bosom . . . attractions which contrasted badly with an ungainly

---

* Similar to the Duchy of Cornwall, which is the hereditary property of the Princes of Wales.

† The Duke without Savoy.

‡ Marie de Medici was also the Princess of Tuscany.

(left) Maximilien, Duc de Sully *(right)* Henriette d'Entragues, mistress of Henry IV

Attempted assassination of Henry IV by Jean Chastel

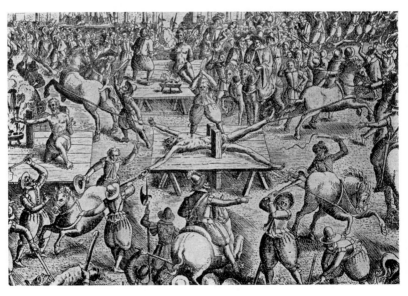

The execution of François Ravaillac, the assassin of Henry IV

figure, large round unexpressive eyes, rude gestures and an incurable vulgarity. Rarely did a face so faithfully betray its owner's
character. One look was enough to show that Her Majesty was
foolish, violent, obstinate, bad-tempered and lazy.

On 5th October her marriage to the King of France was
performed in Florence by proxy as he was unable to be present,
being still detained in Savoie, but it was not until 17th November that she embarked at the port of Leghorn amidst great
pomp and ceremony and set sail for Marseilles.

Her arrival there a few days later, however, contrasted most
unfavourably with her departure from Italy, for there was no
one there to meet her. Her husband had written to apologize
for being unable to be present owing to the fact that he could
not leave his troops who were within sight of victory. Nevertheless she rightly expected that someone else would be there
to meet her on his behalf. She had arrived at Marseilles with
a suite of 1,200, and no arrangements had been made for
her journey to Lyons, where the King intended to receive
her.

Meanwhile Henriette d'Entragues, who four months earlier
had given birth to a stillborn son, thus releasing Henry from
his promise to marry her, followed him to Savoie, much as
Gabrielle had done when he left Paris on 12th March 1596
to attack Amiens. He received news early in October, when
he was in Grenoble, where he had his headquarters, that
she had arrived at the Château de la Cote St André, which
was only a few miles away. The King spent the night with
her there, and next morning she returned with him to Grenoble,
where they lived together until the end of October when
Henriette returned to Paris.

After a long and uncomfortable journey in terrible weather,
the new Queen arrived in Lyons on 3rd December just as
night was falling, but the King had not yet arrived and did
not do so until six days later. He went straight to the Archbishop's Palace, where the Queen was staying and was shown
to her room. He knocked on the door, which was opened by
the dowager Duchesse de Nemours who had been appointed
lady-in-waiting, and asked if he could be allowed to see her.
The Queen told her lady-in-waiting to let him in, and he
spent the night with her. It was doubtless due to the King's

reputation as regard the feminine sex* that so many lurid
accounts of what happened that night behind closed doors
have been handed down and elaborated over the years, but
their authors must have relied entirely on their imagination
for no-one but the King and Queen can have known the true
facts. It would be safe to assume, however, that the marriage
was consummated.

In any event the Queen does not appear to have had anything to complain about, for she wrote to her uncle, the Grand
Duke of Tuscany, three days afterwards to let him know that
"the first contacts with her husband" had given her complete
satisfaction. "I cannot begin to tell you", she wrote, "of the
honour and respect with which His Majesty treats me or of
the kindness which he has shown to me on every occasion."

On 17th December a religious ceremony was held in Lyons
in order that the royal marriage could receive the blessing of
the Church, which was quite unnecessary as the marriage
service by proxy in Florence had been performed according
to the rites of the Catholic Church. The King, however,
insisted on it because he wanted his own people to be able to
take part in the general rejoicing. The same papal legate who
had performed the ceremony in Florence did so in Lyons.

The royal couple stayed in Lyons some time before leaving
for Paris, as the King did not want to be too far away from
Savoie where peace negotiations were going on with the
Duc de Savoie, the papal legate acting as an intermediary.
A treaty was signed on 17th January after a compromise had
been arranged. The Duc de Savoie was allowed to keep
the Marquisat de Saluces but handed over the province of
Bresse and the country surrounding the city of Lyons.

Arrangements were made for the Queen's journey to Paris.
On the King's instructions it was to be done by easy stages
because she was already pregnant, and he said that she should
not overtire herself. He would leave earlier as he wanted to
get to Paris quickly so as to make all the necessary arrangements
for her reception when she entered the capital for the first
time as Queen. His real reason for wanting to get to Paris
before her, however, was quite a different one. He had been

* One of Henry's most popular nicknames was *Le Vert Galant*, the
"dashing ladies' man."

faithful to her for six long weeks, which was a record, and he was longing to see Henriette again. He reached Paris by forced marches and was able to spend a week with her, after which he went to Fontainebleau so that he could join the Queen and be with her when she entered Paris. The week with Henriette had been productive for, according to Cheverny, he left the Marquise de Verneuil as pregnant as he had left his Queen in Lyons.

On 7th January Henry IV and his Queen made their entry into Paris. With the campaign in Savoie over and the rest of France finally pacified, the King was able to realize his one ambition, the restoration of France's unity and economy. During the last ten years of his life he achieved this. He rightly became known as Henry the Great, and he has gone down in history with Charlemagne, Joan of Arc and St Louis as one of France's greatest heroes.

11 The corner stone is laid

THERE was not a single part of France which had not been affected by the Wars of Religion. As the King told the notables of Rouen, "you know to your cost, as I do to mine that when God called me to this crown I found France not only half ruined but almost entirely lost to the French. . . . Through my care and toil I have saved the heritage; I shall now save it from ruin."

There was much to be done. Over 4 million men, women and children had lost their lives, many towns and villages had been plundered and some razed to the gound, and hundreds of thousands of hectares of crops had been ruined. "There was destruction everywhere," wrote the Venetian Ambassador, "a great part of the cattle have disappeared, so that ploughing is no longer possible. The people are not what they used to be, courteous and honest, war and the sight of blood have made them sly, coarse and barbarous."

There was no money left in the Treasury, and the majority of the people of France whether they were bourgeois, workers or peasants were practically penniless. Crime was widespread. In the Languedoc, for example, bands of brigands roamed the countryside pillaging village after village, and even some of the noblemen of France committed highway robbery.

Henry IV found himself faced, therefore, with a task which to many would have seemed hopeless, but he was not daunted by its magnitude, for he possessed natural gifts and a wealth of personal experience which enabled him to set France on her feet again. Although his private life left much to be desired, he was one of the wisest kings who ever sat on the throne of France, and he rarely made the same mistake twice. He also understood the ordinary people and their problems and had a great eye for detail. He believed in absolute monarchy for, as he once said, "a king is only responsible to his

God and his conscience." Nevertheless he was convinced that sovereign power should only be used for the people's good. He also took care to impress this on his ministers and the provincial governors. "Take unceasing care of my people," he told them, "for they are my children. God has committed them in my charge and I am responsible to him for them." Not only did he understand his subjects, but they also got to know and respect him. He loved the peasants and once said that he hoped "to see a chicken in their pots every Sunday."

He had always disliked the life at court, ever since he was virtually imprisoned in the Louvre for several years after the death of his mother, and he spent much of his time travelling all over France, especially through the rural districts, talking to everyone he met in a friendly way. "All my predecessors cared about," he said, "was how much a teston* was worth. I am more interested in finding out how much a fried steak costs and how difficult it is for these poor people to get one."

Although he believed that it was for him to govern France and that he alone was responsible for her fate, and for that reason never called the States General together, he made no important decisions without first consulting his council of ministers, although he did not necessarily always follow their advice. Nevertheless, it gave him the opportunity of hearing other peoples' views before finally making up his own mind.

Now that he was back in Paris and married to a Queen who was soon to provide him with an heir to the throne, the King had time to look around him and see the devastation and chaos that had once been a prosperous France. He quickly realized that the three most important things to be done were to restore the sovereign power, social order and the country's economy, which alone could form a firm foundation upon which a new prosperous and powerful France could be re-built.

To achieve this he relied principally on his friend of long standing, Maximilien de Bethune, whom he created the Duc de Sully. Sully knew Henry's weaknesses as well as his strength and never quite trusted him. They frequently had differences, and Sully opposed many of the King's projects, some of which proved to be extremely effective, but once a decision had been made, even if it were against Sully's advice, he did his best to

* An old French coin.

make the policy work. Nevertheless, between them they gave France ten years of peace, and the country always remembered it as the 'golden age'.

The King established a number of advisory councils, but the one which he consulted most frequently, and always when he wanted to discuss any matter which was of great importance or secrecy, was called the 'Conseil des Affaires', to which only his intimate confidents were admitted, Sully, Jeannin, who was its chairman, Pomponne de Bellievre, Sillery and the most able of his secretaries of State, Villeroy. It was this body which really constituted the Government. Its meetings usually took place, if it was not raining, in the garden of the Louvre, where Henry liked to take his morning exercise.

There were also four Secretaries of State, but their title was purely nominal. From the time of Henry II their sole responsibility had been to ensure that the King's commands were duly carried out by the provincial governors in the areas for which they were responsible. They continued to do this in Henry IV's reign, but he had already begun to allot them other duties and had appointed Villeroy to be in charge of foreign affairs.

The King was not content with merely restoring the sovereign power; he tried to extend it by limiting the powers of the provincial governors, and, although he told the Parlements that he intended to give them more authority than they had ever had previously, he made it quite clear that he expected them to accept any decision he made 'for the good of the State'. He was determined to be the master, and the best way he could achieve this was by centralizing the power of government in Paris. He therefore restricted the powers of the provincial governors and the municipal authorities, and in some of the large towns he even manipulated the local elections by telling the electors whom they should choose as their mayors and aldermen, and when these had been elected he ordered them to appoint his own nominee as governor.

By the end of 1600, having overcome all opposition, he had the reins in his hand, and could have said, with even more justification than Louis XIV *"L'Etat-c'est moi"*.*

* "The State – I am the State." Many historians assert that, in fact Louis XIV never made this remark.

12 The royal court

BEFORE his return to Paris after the campaign in Savoie Henry IV had promised himself a period of leisure to compensate for the 'vexations, fatigue, perils and angers' which he had experienced since he was a child.

Although he was a man of simple tastes and detested the artificiality of court life as he had seen it under the last four Valois kings, the Louvre remained much as it had been in the past, and his servants, his retinue of pages, equerries and aides-de-camp, and a host of hangers-on numbered not less than 1,500. Nevertheless the general atmosphere at the Louvre was much less formal than in earlier reigns, and there was little or no protocol. The King was always accessible, and it is said that his intimate friends could enter his bedroom at any time after he had woken up without first asking his permission and converse with him, even though he was still in bed with the Queen.

As a royal palace, however, the Louvre was more sumptuous than it had ever been before. Beautiful tapestries from the King's château at Pau now adorned the walls of the royal apartments, and Marie de Medici had brought with her from Florence masses of priceless furniture and valuable works of art, most of which were utterly lost on Henry, who preferred the open air and escaped from the stuffy atmosphere of the palace whenever the opportunity arose. Sully, who kept an eagle eye on all the extravagances of the court because he had to pay for them out of the Privy purse, described in his memoirs what were the King's favourite pastimes.

What he liked to do most was to take violent exercise such as riding on horseback at which he was very adept, and practising the use of the weapons with which he was most expert, such as a sword, an arquebus, a pike or a halberd. . . . He also enjoyed running, jumping and swimming and his favourite game was tennis. But most of all he adored hunting.

He had hunted ever since he was a small boy and this was why he had always stayed at the Château de Nerac whenever possible for the surrounding country abounded with deer and wild boar.

Although the Louvre meant very little to him except as somewhere to live, he took a great interest in the city of Paris itself and spent large sums of money in improving it. He had an eye for architecture and was a first-class amateur town planner. Sully thought that much of this expense was unnecessary, but if the King had not insisted Paris would have been the loser, as the Place Dauphine, the two charming pavilions near the Pont-Neuf, the Pont-Neuf itself, the Place Royale (now the Place des Vosges), the Palais du Luxembourg and many other lovely buildings owe their existence to Henry IV's determination to make the city more beautiful.

Until the year 1600 Paris consisted for the most part of untidy blocks of rambling houses divided by small streets and alleys, and it was practically impossible to see the river Seine except when crossing the bridges over it. The King completely changed the face of the city, widened the streets and made some of the boulevards, and he did not do it all from behind his desk. He took a great personal interest in the reconstruction and enjoyed riding round to see how the work was going on and talking to the masons and the landscape gardeners who were doing it. He also made tremendous improvements to the Louvre and the Château de Fontainebleau, one of the most lovely buildings in the whole of France.

He devoted far more of his time to making these improvements than he did to his personal appearance. Although the contemporary portraits and engravings of the King invariably depict him wearing satin doublets, silk stockings and velvet capes, he was usually dressed quite differently except, of course, on State occasions. The Venetian Ambassador said that he was always in such a hurry to get out of doors in the morning that he could never even spare the time to dress himself properly and frequently appeared with his doublet unbuttoned and his stockings not properly fastened. When, on one occasion, he was taken to task by one of the Queen's ladies-in-waiting for being so slovenly dressed, he said, "I am always being criticized for something. Some do so because I like beautiful buildings and spend too much money on them," doubtless referring to Sully. "Others because I play cards and throw dice. Some, because I spend so much of my time hunting, others, because I am fond of tent-pegging*, and some because I enjoy giving banquets and balls."

The only thing that made life bearable at the Louvre, apart from flirting with the court beauties, was that he was surrounded by many of his most intimate friends, many of whom had known him since he was a boy. Among them were Sully, Aubigné, Montmorency, Duplessis de Mornay, La Noue, Bassompierre and Bellegarde.

Sully was the King's guide, philosopher and friend and is as well known to students of French history as Cardinal de Richelieu, who carried on after Henry's death the great work which Sully had done to restore France to prosperity and power. Although Sully's influence upon the King was considerable, he was seven years his junior. He had been brought up as a Protestant and when only 13 years of age had narrowly escaped being massacred on the eve of St Bartholomew's day. When Henry, as King of Navarre, made his escape from the Louvre and Catherine de Medici in 1576, Sully went with him and since then had hardly ever left his side. The King and he had many differences, and one of them occurred when Sully succeeded in preventing Henry from marrying Gabreille d'Estrées, but despite it all he remained loyal to his sovereign until the end and never lost Henry's confidence and affection. When Henry IV was assassinated, Sully was overcome with grief, but at the Queen's request carried on as Surintendant des Finances† until his resignation eleven months later. He never returned to the Court but lived in retirement until he died in 1642 at the age of 82.

Aubigné, who was three years Henry's senior, was unlike the King's other friends. He was both a poet and a classical scholar and, it is said, translated Plato's *Criton* from the original

* The French equivalent was 'Courses de Bagues'. A ring was used instead of a tent-peg.
† Chancellor of the Exchequer.

Greek when only 8 years old. He came to the Louvre in 1575, just before Henry escaped, and it was he who had advised him to do so. From then until Henry's abjuration Aubigné was one of his advisers until the King made peace with The League. Aubigné did not agree and left, but many years afterwards returned to the court and remained there until the King's assassination. Before he himself died in Geneva twenty years later he said that Henry was the greatest King France had ever known. "Doubtless he was not without faults but he possessed virtues which were truly sublime."

Montmorency, unlike Aubigné, was not a man of culture but a simple soldier, and held the appointment of Constable of France. The King referred to him as "My Constable who cannot read." But he was a fine horseman and a keen huntsman and that brought them both together.

Of the other four, the Duc de Bellegarde had had the most interesting career. He came from an impoverished family which lived in the south of France, and joined the Court of Henry III where, after holding two junior appointments, he became master of the King's Horse. Although he was a Catholic, he joined up with Henry IV when he succeeded his brother-in-law, became one of his most intimate friends and remained so even after Henry discovered that Bellegarde was sharing the favours of Gabrielle d'Estrées whom he had first introduced to the King. In spite of this he never lost Henry's confidence, for it was Bellegarde who was sent to Florence to act as proxy for the King at his marriage with Marie de Medici.

With these seven men around him there was always something to talk about. The debauchery of Henry III's court, the machinations of 'La Serpente', the massacre of St Bartholomew, their experiences during the religious wars and the successful campaigns after the King's accession. They had shared his perils and his defeats and were now able to share his triumph.

While Henry IV was, therefore, able to enjoy the company of his friends at court, the Queen's life was extremely unhappy, for he was an impossible husband. The Duc de Cheverny, in his memoirs, stated that from the commencement of their marriage the royal couple had a great love and respect for each other, but as far as the King was concerned nothing could be further from the truth. Their life together was nothing but a long series of wrangles and disputes, and almost immediately after the Queen's arrival at the Louvre she learned that during their engagement Henry had entered into an agreement to marry Henriette d'Entragues and that while she was travelling from Lyons to Paris he had spent a week with the Marquise and made her pregnant. Nevertheless she had not expected that he would add insult to injury by bringing Henriette to the Louvre and presenting her to the Queen, yet this is what he did, and in front of everybody. "This woman," he told her, "has been my mistress and now wishes to be your humble servant." He should not, however, have used the past tense as she was still his mistress.

Henriette inclined her head to kiss the Queen's dress, but as she did not bend her knee as the etiquette demanded, Henry roughly pushed her forward until her head nearly touched the floor. The Queen showed great self control and allowed Henriette to have an apartment at the Louvre so the King was in future able to have his wife, his mistress and his bastards living under the same roof.

But even the Queen and Henriette did not satisfy his lust, and it was not long before he offered Mademoiselle de la Bourdeissière, one of the Queen's maids-of-honour, 50,000 livres in return for her favours. Meanwhile the court was able to watch with some amusement the Queen and the King's mistress getting larger every day and wonder which of them would be the first to be confined. As was to be expected, for few of them had not heard of the King's visit to Henriette in the previous January, the Queen won the race, but only by a short head. Marie de Medici gave birth to a son, who one day was to become Louis XIII, and five weeks later Henriette also presented the King with a son, thus fulfilling his prophecy that between them they would bear him 'a master and a valet'. History was to repeat itself almost a year later, when the Queen and the Marquise both gave birth to daughters within two months of each other.

Nevertheless, the King felt no shame whatsoever and even boasted that there were four other women in Paris who were also pregnant by him at the same time, and when the Queen reproached him for having so many mistresses he told her that he loved her as his wife, whereas he loved the others merely because of the pleasure they gave him. The birth of a son to Henriette, however, had revived her ambition to be the Queen of France, for she said that while her rival only had a son she had the Dauphin. But it was not until three years later that she became involved in a plot with the Duc d'Auvergne, her father, and the Duc de Bouillon to proclaim her son as heir presumptive to the throne in place of the Dauphin.

13 The Biron conspiracy

Among the King's friends there was a Judas, Maréchal Biron. It was he who once told his father, the Maréchal Biron who was killed during the siege of Epernay, that if he had been in Henry's shoes he would have had him shot.

Biron had been the King's ablest general, and he was the last person in the world that Henry imagined would become a traitor. He had been appointed governor of Burgundy and created Duc de Biron but still had greater ambitions. He had been born a Catholic but was later brought up by his aunt, Madame de Brisambourg, as a Protestant, but in 1601 he secretly became the leader of the few remaining influential Catholics, most of whom were members of The League. In 1602 he joined in with Spain and the Duc de Savoie in a conspiracy to assassinate the King, and at the same time get rid of the Dauphin and the other princes of the blood so that there would be no heir presumptive to the throne of France. According to Biron's plan, the Duc de Savoie, once the King was dead, would invade the Dauphiné and Provence; the King of Spain would seize the Languedoc, the Guyenne and Brittany; Biron would take over Burgundy and the Franche-Comté and Henriette's bastard son by Henry would be proclaimed king of France.

The King was informed of the details of the plot while he was in Blois through a secret agent named La Fin, who was able to give him the full dossier, which included several original documents incriminating Biron, and he consulted the Duc d'Epernon and the Duc de Bouillon and asked for their advice. Both of them assured Henry that they knew nothing of the plan and that, in any event, now that he had been warned of the danger there was no need for him to worry as

he could take the necessary steps to circumvent it. A report
of their meeting with the King at Blois must have been given
to Biron by Epernon and Bouillon, for he wrote to the King
and asked him where he had got his information. The King
by way of reply reassured Biron and told him that nothing
could please him more than for Biron to come to Fontainebleau
and confirm his loyalty.

On receipt of Henry's letter Biron, after thinking it over very
carefully, decided to go and see the King and arrived at the
court on 13th June. Henry received him and said that it was
wise of him to come, otherwise a full investigation of the
allegations against Biron would have had to be made. The
King took him into the château gardens, told him what he
had heard, and urged him for his own good to tell the truth.
Biron, who pretended to be surprised at the King's attitude,
said that he had no need to ask for pardon as he had committed no offence. After lunch Henry again interviewed Biron
and insisted that he should come out into the open and tell
him everything, but the *maréchal* said nothing except to demand
that the King should give the names of his accusers. By this
time the King was convinced that La Fin had told him the
truth and decided to have Biron and the Duc d'Auvergne,
who was also implicated, arrested, but before doing so he asked
Biron to come and see him that evening. When he arrived
Henry made one last attempt to get Biron to confess, but in
vain. He then said goodbye to him, but as Biron was walking
through the ante-chamber after taking leave of the King he
was arrested by the captain of the royal guard and taken to
the Bastille.

He was brought to trial before the Court of Parlement but
the members were loth to convict him solely upon the testi-
mony of La Fin and the documentary evidence which he
produced, and adjourned for further evidence. Fortunately
another of the conspirators, who had been kept under lock
and key by the Duc de Savoie who thought that he might
offer himself as a witness for the Crown, managed to escape
and when called as witness by the Procureur-General confirmed
the evidence of La Fin.

On 23rd June Biron again appeared before the Court of
Parlement to give evidence for his defence. He admitted

having made disloyal remarks about the King but nothing more, and then made a short speech in mitigation. "If I have spoken evil," he told the court, "I have always acted honourably. . . . The judges who hold the scales of justice, before deciding what punishment I should receive for having spoken foolishly without any malicious intent, should take into consideration all that I have done to serve the State."

He was, however, convicted of treason and sentenced to death, his execution being carried out on 29th July. Nevertheless, under the pretext of saving him the humiliation of a public execution, the King gave orders that the sentence should be carried out inside the Bastille; but this was not the real reason for so doing. It was feared that a public execution might give rise to a demonstration of sympathy on the part of the crowd, and the King was most anxious to avoid such a thing happening, and he was undoubtedly right. The trial had created quite a stir in Paris, and by some people Biron was regarded as a Christian martyr and defender of the Catholic faith.

14 An ill-assorted couple

HENRY's relations with his Queen did not improve but worsened as time went on. She had every reason to be annoyed but made no attempt to hide her feelings. Except when they having a violent quarrel, he always treated her with consideration and respect, and he thought that she ought to be satisfied with that and make allowances for his many indiscretions. He told Sully on one occasion that his greatest desire was to live with her in an atmosphere of friendship, peace and mutual understanding, but that he and his wife were obviously quite incompatible for whenever he said something she immediately contradicted him. He also complained that she spent her whole time grumbling and sulking and especially when he came back to the palace after a day's hunting, when all he wanted to do was to give her a kiss and tell her all about the day's sport, but was greeted with a frosty look. She used to fly into a temper at the slightest pretext and when they started shouting at each other almost everyone in the palace could hear what was going on.

When the King was away, however, her whole attitude changed, and she found much to amuse her, but although she was the Queen of France she felt that she had come down in the world. She found the French court extremely dull and shoddy after the gay and luxurious life she had led in Florence. Her 'smelly soldier', as she called Henry, she found most distasteful, and the Louvre was so packed with officers and members of the King's guard that to her it was more like a barracks than a palace. She even hated the Louvre itself, and shortly after she came to live in it she described it in a letter which she wrote to her uncle the Grand Duke of Tuscany as "half ruined, half built, half antique and half modern."

The interior of the Louvre, however, she had been able to change by filling it with Italian furniture, valuable pictures and magnificent tapestries, all of which the King disliked intensely—although he appreciated beautiful things—because they reminded him of Catherine de Medici.

There were other complications. Having been brought up as a member of a family of bankers in an atmosphere of wealth and luxury, she had most extravagant tastes. She wore so many necklaces, brooches and rings that she looked like a jeweller's model, and she was always asking for more. One of her pearl necklaces had been given to her as a present from the King, and it had cost the earth. Nor was this all. She had also contracted many debts, and when the King was persuaded by Sully not to settle them she told everyone that she had not come all the way from Italy to become a beggar.

The King might have put up with all her tantrums if only she had been intelligent enough to take some interest in what he was trying to do – to bring happiness and prosperity to his subjects, an ambition which was so dear to his heart – but whenever he tried to tell her about his schemes the Queen immediately changed the subject.

There were many people at the Court who though they admired and respected Henry as their King could not condone his loose way of living, but they also criticized the Queen for not trying to make the best of things and could not forget the old saying that 'it takes two to make a quarrel'.

In the spring of 1603 the King was taken seriously ill and thought that he was going to die. He made a fairly rapid recovery, however, but during his illness he had plenty of time to take stock of himself, to reflect on the past and to make plans for the future in the event of his death.

The Queen could not help feeling sorry for him and spent many hours by his bedside. On one of these occasions he told her that he prayed God he would get well again and promised that if he did she would in future be obeyed and respected. He also took steps to ensure that should he die the Queen would become Regent during the minority of his son the Dauphin. He also appointed her as a member of his Council and briefed her about his plans for the restoration of France.

Henriette's reaction to her lover's illness was as commend-

L

able as it was unexpected. She went to see the Queen and offered her hand in friendship. The Queen seemed genuinely moved and graciously accepted the offer, saying that if Henriette wanted a reconciliation she would love her not only as a good companion and friend but as her own sister.

15 The Entragues conspiracy

THE reconciliation between the Queen and Henriette did not last for long, and, as far as the latter was concerned, it was never intended seriously. All Henriette wanted was to gain time. There would surely come a day when the King's signed promise of marriage could be turned to good account. Should the King die in the near future, and from the state of his health it was not beyond the bounds of possibility, it might be used to persuade the Pope to annul Henry's marriage with Marie de Medici which would make the Dauphin a bastard. What Rome had done could be undone, and the King of Spain* could be relied upon to bring his influence to bear on the Pope. The representatives of Spain at the Court of Henry IV had already promised the support of their government, and Montmorency, who was the Duc d'Auvergne's father-in-law was in the secret.

Auvergne had already been involved in the Biron conspiracy and was arrested only a few hours after Biron and confined in the Bastille with the *maréchal*. The King, however, never had him brought to trial so as not to compromise Henriette, and five weeks after Biron's execution Auvergne was set at liberty.

Meanwhile the famous document had been kept in safe custody by Auvergne and Henriette's father, Balzac d'Entrague and Henriette herself became involved in the conspiracy.

Fortunately the King discovered what was going on through an English spy, named Thomas Mann, who was acting as a double-agent for both Spain and England.

Auvergne and Entragues were both tried by the Court of Parlement and sentenced to death, and Henriette was interrogated by Sully on behalf of the King. Later the sentence of

* Philip III.

death was commuted to imprisonment for life after Entragues had agreed to surrender the compromising document which had led to so much trouble. Henriette was declared innocent, although she had confessed to Sully that all she had done was to assure the future of herself and her children in the event of their father dying.

The Entragues conspiracy had one good result, for Henriette could not remain at court after what had happened. The Queen breathed a sigh of relief, and even the King did not care very much, for Henriette was beginning to pall on him and it would not be difficult for him to find a substitute.

After spending two years in the Bastille Auvergne was set free. Entragues, however, was allowed to go free provided he remained on his property at Verneuil but after a year he was released from this condition.

It was not long before the King found a new mistress, Jacqueline de Bueil, an orphan only 16 years old, who was shortly afterwards created Comtesse de Moret. She knew how to bargain, however, and was not satisfied with merely a title. She also received some land, an income, a present of 30,000 livres and even a husband, named Champvallon, as she inisted on getting married in order to give her respectability. On the night of her marriage, according to L'Estoile, she was allowed to sleep in the same bed as her husband, but some of the King's suite were posted in the bedroom, by his orders, to see that nothing happened. Next morning she went to bed with the King in Paris until two o'clock in the afterroon, during which time poor Champvallon was allowed to lie down on a bed in an attic immediately above the King's room 'so that he could be on top of his wife but with a floor in between'. Jacqueline remained the King's mistress until 1607, during which time she bore him a son whom the King named Antoine de Bourbon.

The Entragues conspiracy had given Queen Margot just the opportunity for which she had been waiting twenty long years. She left the Château d'Usson and suddenly, to everyone's surprise except the King's, arrived at the Louvre. The main object of her visit was to try and get hold of her mother's fortune, which Henry III had given away to the Duc d'Auvergne who was the illegitimate son of Charles IX, but when she wrote to ask Henry's permission to come to Paris she gave as the pretext for wishing to see him the fact that she had certain valuable information about the Duc d'Auvergne who lived quite near her. Henry welcomed the opportunity as he wanted her to come to court so that she could formally pay her respects to the new Queen, to which in the King's opinion, his wife was entitled. Marguerite de Valois had learned a great many things since she had left Nerac and she complied. with the King's wish and was received graciously by the Queen After all they had one thing in common; they both had experience of Henry as a husband, and that alone was enough to give them an affinity for each other.

The ice had been broken from the very start, and it could truly be said that 'they all lived happily ever after'. They spent much of their time together. The King was delighted, and in a letter to one of his friends, Monsieur de la Force, he wrote, "I have here, by my side, my sister Queen Marguerite* who is behaving in such a way that I am more than content." A few days after Marguerite arrived they were all three seen sitting in the Queen's bedroom with the Dauphin. The Queen was still in bed, Henry was sitting beside her with his son who was stroking his dog and Marguerite was on her knees next to them, a charming scene which, had it been depicted by the painter to the Royal Household, would be hanging in the Louvre today. As Monsieur Mariejol has written, "Henry never loved Marguerite so much as he did when he was no longer under an obligation to do so."

---

* It was the custom for the King to refer to his Queen as his sister because she was the daughter of France.

16 The restoration

Biron, Auvergne and Entragues were now out of the way, but the Duc de Bouillon, who had been deeply involved in the conspiracy of 1602 was still free and while he remained so was a positive danger. The King who had previously regarded him as one of most loyal supporters at last realized that something had to be done to put an end to his scheming.

Meanwhile Bouillon had decided, shortly after the discovery of the Biron plot, to leave France and had taken refuge with his brother-in-law in Heidelberg the Elector Palatine, who sent an envoy to see the King and persuade him to take no further action against Bouillon.

Henry, however, refused to listen and told the envoy to inform the Elector that unless his brother-in-law gave himself up and admitted his complicity he would be brought to trial if he ever set foot in France again.

By this time Bouillon had left Heidelberg and returned to Sedan, which his wife Charlotte de Marck had received as her dowry when she married Bouillon, a marriage which had been arranged by the King himself. Realizing the dangerous position he was in, Bouillon sought the King's pardon, but he was too late. Henry was already marching on Sedan with an army of 10,000 French infantry and 6,000 Swiss with the intention of capturing it. Bouillon when he heard of the King's approach said that he would fight to the last ditch, but when he saw that he was so heavily outnumbered he changed his mind and on 2nd April 1606 surrendered. To mark the importance of the occasion the King made a triumphal entry into the town and then withdrew, leaving behind a garrison of fifty under the command of a Huguenot named Nettancourt.

The short campaign now over, Henry returned to Paris

where he received an enthusiastic welcome. He rode through the streets of the city in state and behind him rode the prisoner Bouillon guarded by an escort of cavalry. This, however, was the only punishment which Bouillon received. Once again the King was magnanimous in victory, and two years later Sedan was restored by Henry to its owner.

That was the end of the conspiracies. The throne of France was now safe, though not the King himself, for his life was always in danger. The last four years of his reign, however, were peaceful, and he was able to continue the arduous task of restoring France's power and prosperity, the foundations of which he had already laid. The first and most important task was to try and put the country's finances on a firm footing then, having done that, to improve agriculture, reorganize the manufacturing industries and build up trade.

It was to Sully, whom the King had appointed Surintendant des Finances in 1601, that he entrusted this difficult assignment. The new Chancellor was not popular with the Treasury officials, many of whom had been feathering their nests for some time, and they realized that in future this was not going to be easy. What they disliked most about him was that he had eyes in his head and knew how to say 'No'. One of the first things he did was to take away from Henriette d'Entragues and the Duc de Soissons a privilege which they had obtained to receive a commision, by way of tax, on every bale of cotton imported into France.

Sully also discovered that some of the provincial governors had been imposing taxes on their own authority and that was one of the reasons why the King took away some of their powers.

Many other stringent financial reforms had to be made and, as always happens, those who were most affected by them complained bitterly, and they were, what for want of a better name, could be called 'the upper classes', for the King was determined that the 'people' should not bear the main brunt of the burden. That remained during the whole of his reign an overriding principle and that is why the government of France, although an absolute monarchy, was 'for the people' even though it was not 'by the people'.

The King's first thought was to protect the countryside from violence and prevent damage to the crops, and shortly after the Biron plot he made it illegal for anybody, irrespective of who they were, to carry arms on the highway. He also forbade the country gentlemen hunting in the fields once the corn was in blade and riding through the vineyards from the 1st March until the vintage. He also authorized the parishes to buy back at a reasonable price their common land, which many of them had been obliged to sell in more difficult times.

Being convinced that the best way to increase productivity was to make the work easier, the King encouraged new ideas. Two centuries earlier the production of silk had been started in Provence and especially in the districts around Avignon with considerable success, and Henry saw no reason why it could not be done in other parts of France. He first got the idea after reading a book published in 1599 by a Huguenot whom he knew personally, Olivier de Serres, and his *valet de chambre* was very interested in the project and frequently spoke to his master about it.

After making several enquiries Henry was sure that silk-worms could be raised in most of his provinces and decided to encourage the planting of mulberry trees throughout the country. He made arrangements for all the necessary require-ments to be delivered to Tours, Orleans and Lyons and 16,000 leaflets giving instructions on how to plant the mulberry trees, how to breed and feed the silkworms, how to collect the cocoons and extract the silk from them and process it. Nor was this all. He also sent teams of experts to explain in detail to those who were interested the instructions set out in the leaflet.

The King's scheme could have been a great success, but once it got into the hand of the civil servants it was strangled with red tape. Moreover, instead of granting a bonus to anyone who successfully produced the silk, they had to pay to the Treasury a percentage on every sale they made. The landlords on whose land the peasants planted the mulberry trees also took their commission. When all this had been paid there was very little profit left and it was not worth the trouble and hard work.

Another scheme was set on foot to reclaim large areas of marshy land which then existed in many parts of France, but the King discovered that the French peasants had neither the wish nor the knowledge to do it themselves. He therefore signed a contract with an Englishman named Humphrey Bradley, who lived in Holland, giving him the sole right to drain the marshland. By way of payment Bradley was to be allowed to keep half the land so reclaimed.

The task proved to be extremely difficult and was hampered from the start by the owners of the land – who objected to it being done – and by lack of capital, as Bradley, after making a thorough survey, came to the conclusion that the appropriation of half the land reclaimed would scarcely cover the expense of draining and would leave very little or no profit. By the time the King was assassinated very little had been done, but the way had been laid open and he deserves the credit for the extensive reclamation which was carried out during his son Louis XIII's reign.

He also allowed farmers and wine growers to export wheat and wine, subject to the payment of a tax on all produce they sold abroad. As both these commodities were in abundant supply and exceeded what was required for the home market it was possible to export them without creating a shortage in France. The King also considered that by opening a foreign market it would enable his subjects to obtain a higher price and would also ensure a flow of foreign currency into his kingdom, which would help its economy. At first permission to export wheat and wine was only given to a few of the provinces, but in 1601 it was extended to the whole country without the exporters being liable to pay any tax. In 1604, however, exports to Spain were stopped because the Spanish government decided to put a heavy tax on all French imports by way of reprisal, and in 1608 all exportation of wheat and wine had to be temporarily stopped because of a shortage due to bad weather conditions.

Although the towns had not suffered the same damage as the country districts had during the religious wars, the manufacturing industries had been badly hit. Many of these industries had been practically ruined because of the bad relations between management and employers. The King's government decided that it would help if the corporative system were improved and made obligatory. This was done and an organization was set up to fix the wages of the workers.

To follow up the King's plan to produce silk, factories were built to weave it into fine fabrics, and many other new industries were started to manufacture glass, white lead and make steel out of iron which was in plentiful supply. Many new inventions were submitted for approval, and one contractor undertook to construct a canal between Toulouse and Narbonne in one year at a cost of 40,000 écus.

Sully regarded them all as cranks and gave very stupid reasons for rejecting all their suggestions. He was still living in the past. The silk industry, he said, was quite unsuitable for France because her climate made it impossible to rear silkworms and people who worked in a factory would never make good soldiers. He was also opposed to 'any form of luxury'.

The King told him that he was talking nonsense. "If my people want to have nice things," he said, "without impoverishing my kingdom, then we must make them ourselves."

He continued to encourage the manufacture of what Sully called luxuries and amongst other things revived the tapestry trade for which France had once been famous but which had almost disappeared. During the last ten years of his reign industry was put on its feet again, many new factories were built and in the cities and towns the inhabitants were able to look forward to better times.

With a revival of trade the next important thing to be done was to build new roads and bridges, for adequate means of transport were essential. Many bridges had been destroyed or damaged, and many of the main roads were impassable. To do this was going to cost a lot of money and the Treasury was short of funds. Sully, however, realized that something had to be done and before the end of the reign the situation had greatly improved and new bridges over the Seine, the Marne and the Yonne, and at Toulouse, Grenoble, Soissons, Avignon, Rouen and Orleans had already been built or were under construction, and a canal connecting the Seine with the Loire was well under way.

Efforts were also made to increase exports. Until 1603 Spain had been France's best customer but the bad relations between the two countries, which still existed and had worsened after the abortive Biron conspiracy, were again revealed when Philip III imposed a heavy import duty on all goods coming from France – which Henry IV countered by a similar tax on all Spanish goods. As this reprisal had no effect Henry decided to ban all trade between the two countries, but to his great embarrassment he later had to withdraw the ban as he discovered that the English had seized the opportunity of buying goods from France and transporting them to Spain. James I of England was then negotiating peace with Philip and had offered to mediate on behalf of France, as a result of which the French Ambassador in London signed a treaty with Spain in which the Spaniards agreed to lower the rate of duty. Three years later a somewhat similar treaty was signed with England, but neither of them produced any tangible result as the contraband trade with Spain was still carried on unmolested by pirate ships.

Nevertheless, France was already exporting her goods to many other parts of the world and, under Henry IV began to expand her foreign trade. She tried to compete with the Dutch in the Far East and the King formed an organization somewhat similar to the East India Company for this purpose.

Morocco opened its doors to French goods and a colony was founded on the St Lawrence at Quebec which the King's successors were eventually unable to retain. It was intended to be the foundation of a large French Empire in North America. France also held other parts of the east coast of America which today form the States of New York, Connecticut, Massachusetts, New Hampshire and Maine.

It was in Henry IV's reign that the idea became rooted which has since been the guiding theme of all French colonization. He saw no reason why the natives of a colony should be either exterminated or enslaved, nor why they should not enjoy the same liberties and privileges as the French colonials who lived among them.

Having had bitter experience of the chaos and disaster which hatred, intolerance and bigotry can bring in its train Henry was determined that it should never happen again. He had seen the whole of France torn apart and families divided, violence and lawlessness everywhere, the countryside laid waste, towns and villages left almost in ruins. If there was one thing to be done it was to maintain religious tolerance. Why should Christians who worshipped the same God fight each other because they did so in a different way?

The French Protestants had very little cause to complain for in no country in Europe was a religious minority better treated than in France. Nevertheless, Henry made it quite clear to the Catholics that he intended to maintain the rights and privileges which the Protestants had obtained by the Edict of Nantes. To keep the balance of power, however, when the circumstances made it necessary at any time to make a concession to either of the two Churches he gave something to the other by way of compensation. For example when he allowed the Jesuits to return to France eight years after they had been banished from the country when it was discovered that they had been implicated in the attempted assassination of the King by Chastel, he extended the period for which the Protestants had been allowed, under the provisions of the Edict of Nantes, to keep certain strongholds and permitted them to strengthen the defences of La Rochelle which was their main base.

There was great surprise throughout France when the King decided to let the Jesuits come back, for very few people really wanted them. The Protestants naturally regarded them as their deadly enemy, the Parlement was opposed to their return, the majority of Frenchmen suspected them of being hand in glove with Spain, and even the Catholics themselves were quite prepared to do without them.

The Pope had, for some time, been trying to persuade the King to end their exile, but he had persistently refused. Nevertheless he was now beginning to think that the Catholic Church had need of them for it had gradually been falling into a very bad state. The kings of France had for many years been filling the Church with bishops who had no real qualifications whatsoever but happened to come from good families. Most of them were gentlemen of the court and lived far away from their dioceses and enjoyed many perquisites. The Cardinal de Joyeuse, for example, who was first Archbishop of Toulouse and was then transferred to Rouen, owned six abbeys. Many of the religious orders were corrupt, many abbeys had no abbots and many bishoprics had no bishops.

Moreover the morals of the parish priests, which were bad enough before the religious wars, had become even worse.

The King had been trying to improve this state of affairs for some time, and thought that the Jesuits who, whatever else might be said of them, were the intellectual cream of the clergy would have a steadying influence on the Church and would be able to help him raise the standard of education which he regarded as of the greatest importance.

Meanwhile the King's private life had not changed. Shortly after the Queen had given birth to a daughter in January 1606 he renewed his liaison with Henriette, who had been in touch with him by correspondence since she had been forced to leave the Louvre at the time of the Entragues conspiracy. He had not allowed her son and daughter to leave with her, and they remained at St Germain-en-Laye, where they were brought up together with the children of the Queen and Gabrielle, much to the Queen's disgust – but her feelings when Henriette reappeared on the scene were even stronger. She wrote to her uncle saying, "This woman has only one aim in life – to insult and torture me." Henry's other affairs did not upset her so much and she had come to regard them as part of the day's work, which was just as well for there were still more to come.

Henriette's return, however, did not affect his life so far as Jacqueline de Bueil was concerned. He refused to be separated from her and before long had taken yet another mistress, Charlotte des Essarts, Comtesse de Romorantin, who soon bore him a daughter who also went to join the kindergarten at St Germain-en-Laye.

The relations between Henry and his Queen had by now become impossible. He had discovered that she too was not altogether blameless, though not without justification, but that did not worry him greatly. When, however, she interfered to save Mademoiselle de Fonlebon from his famous amorous advances he told Sully that he intended to banish her to some château in the provinces or have her taken back to Italy with everything she had brought with her. Sully managed to dissuade him from doing anything so foolish. He told Henry that he should think first of his children, and that it was the duty of a King to put his throne before his pleasure. "The only way to get the better of an obstinate and bad-tempered woman," he said, "is by being patient." The situation shortly became easier, however, when there was an unexpected reconciliation, or at least a peaceful co-existence, between the Queen and Henriette, which either coincided with or was responsible for a cooling off on the part of the King towards his favourite, who once again left the court and returned to Verneuil.

Although Henry was not a good husband he was an excellent father, which was fortunate as he had many children and they were a very mixed bag. The thirteen children who were brought up together at St Germain-en-Laye had five different mothers. The Queen had borne him six, Gabrielle d'Estrées three and Henriette d'Entragues two. The son of Jacqueline de Bueil and the daughter of Charlotte des Essarts made up the party. The King, however, loved them all equally, whether legitimate or not and he spent a lot of time with them.

He was also very strict and believed in the old saying, 'spare the rod and spoil the child'. He remembered the spartan way in which he had been brought up and always said that an occasional beating had never done him any harm. One afternoon just as he was caning the Dauphin, who was an extremely wilful boy, the Queen came into the room. She was very annoyed and said, "You never treat your bastards like that," to which he replied "My bastards can always be punished by the Dauphin if they are naughty, but who is going to punish the Dauphin if I don't myself?"

On two other occasions when Henry beat the Dauphin for firing a pistol loaded with blank ammunition at one of the courtiers who had annoyed him, and for smashing in the head of a sparrow, the Queen once again objected. "Pray God, Madame," he said, "I live a long time for my son will ill-treat you when I am gone," a prophecy that was later to come true.

During the last ten years of his reign when the King's main objective was the restoration of France he had many other problems on his hands which affected France's relations with other European powers.

The Treaty of Vervins, which had brought the religious wars to an end, had not settled other difficulties with Spain and Austria, which were mainly due to the fact that the Hapsburgs and the Spanish monarchy had family connections.

The daughter of Maximilian II, Anne-Marie, had married Philip II and was the mother of Philip III, who at this time sat on the throne of Spain. Maximilian's son Rudolph had succeeded his father as Emperor of Austria in 1576 and had taken stern measures against the Protestants.

In Italy, Spain, which held Naples, Sicily and Sardinia, not only dominated the west coast but, as they also possessed Milan, the Spaniards barred the route to France. What was Henry to do about it? He could not even dream of going to war with Spain under the conditions which existed at that time, even had it served any useful purpose, for on what allies could he rely for help against Austria which, in the event of his declaring war, would immediately have come in on the side of Spain?

As for the Protestants of Germany, they were divided. The Dutch could hardly look after their own interests let alone continue to fight against Spain, which still controlled a large part of the Low Countries. England was still at war with Spain, or, to be more accurate, was harassing the Spanish navy on the high seas, and in any event Henry IV knew by experience that Elizabeth was unlikely to risk either her country's money or its army by taking part in a war on the continent of Europe.

Did he dare make overtures to Spain? There were, it is true, many influential people in France who would have been glad to see an *entente cordiale* between the two countries. They included most of the former Leaguers, the Guises, the Duc de Mayenne, the Duc d'Epernon and the Catholic hierarchy, but to enter into an alliance with Spain would mean abandoning the Dutch, a rupture with the Protestants in Germany, and losing touch with Italy. What is more it would have meant the end of France's traditional policy of maintaining natural frontiers.

There was, however, another possible solution to the problem, namely to carry on a cold war with Spain and in that way, without actually going to war, cause much harm to the Spaniards without weakening France herself. It would also have another advantage: the King would have more time in which to restore the country's finances and put his army on a war footing, before embarking on another war.

Henry IV therefore decided to adopt the latter course, but a few months before his assassination he had changed his mind and was considering an idea of Sully's known as the 'Grand Design'.*

Something on the lines of the 'Grand Design' had been in Henry IV's mind ever since the Treaty of Vervins in 1598, when he had first explored its possibilities with Queen Elizabeth and later with James I. The intention was to enter into an alliance with England, Scotland, Sweden and Denmark to help the Dutch by conquering the Spanish Netherlands. The Swiss were to take over the Franche-Comté. the Tyrol and Alsace. It was also proposed to do away with the Hapsburg Empire and give Bohemia and Hungary the right to elect their own king, to drive the Spaniards out of Flanders and Italy to the Spanish peninsular behind the Pyrenees, where they would cease to be a threat to their neighbours.

Having freed Europe Henry proposed to organize it into fifteen different states, a kind of United States of Europe envisaged three centuries later by Aristide Briand twelve times Prime Minister of France.

These states were to consist of:
(1) Six hereditary monarchies: France, Spain, England, Sweden, Denmark and Lombardy.
(2) Six monarchies whose kings would be elected†: Rome, Venice, Austria, Poland, Hungary and Bohemia.
(3) Three Federal Republics: Helvetia (consisting of Switzerland, Franche-Comté, the Tryol and Alsace), Belgium (consisting of Holland and the Spanish Netherlands) and Italy (excluding Rome, Naples and Venice).

Europe was to be Christian, and only three religions would be recognized: Catholic, Lutheran and Calvinist.

'The barbarous Moscovites and the infidel Turks' were to be excluded.

All disputes between the various States were to be settled by an organization on the lines of the League of Nations called the General Council.

The 'Grand Design' was nothing if not grandiose, but it was in those days a Utopian dream. Similar attempts have

* *Le Grand Dessein.*
† As the Kings of Poland already were.

been made in more recent times, on a much wider scale, to provide a substitute for world government first by creating the League of Nations and secondly by the United Nations Organization. The first of these was a dismal failure, and it is still too early to decide whether the second will prove to be more effective.

17 The last fifteen months

It was towards the end of 1608 that Charlotte de Montmorency, the daughter of the Constable of France*, first made her appearance at the Louvre, blissfully unaware of the fate that awaited her. She was very beautiful and only 15 years old, but within a few weeks of her arrival she had become engaged to Bassompierre and the wedding was to take place at the end of January 1609. It was postponed, however, by the intervention of the Duc de Bouillon, who was Montmorency's nephew and objected to the marriage. On 16th January the King saw her for the first time when she took the part of a nymph in a sumptuous ballet organized by the Queen and immediately fell in love with her; but on the following day he had an attack of gout which had been troubling him for some time and had to stay in bed.

One morning while he was still in bed thinking of Charlotte he sent a message to Bassompierre ordering him to come to the King's apartment. As soon as he arrived Henry told the young man, who was only 29 years of age that he was in love with his fiancée and begged him to break off the engagement.

In his memoirs Bassompierre described the interview.

After sighing deeply, His Majesty spoke to me, "I am madly in love with Madamoiselle de Montmorency," he said. "If you marry her and she loves you I will hate you. If she loves me you will hate me. It would be a pity if this were to happen and destroy our friendship for I am very fond of you and have a great respect for you. I am, therefore, determined to marry her to my nephew, the Prince de Condé, and keep her in the family for this will be a consolation to me in my old age which is already upon me. I shall give to my nephew, who is young and much prefers hunting to

* "My Constable who cannot read." See page 154.

women, a hundred thousand francs so that he can have a good time while I have her love and affection without taking advantage of it."

On 17th May 1609 Condé and Charlotte were married. The King never left her alone and showered her with favours, but to his surprise and disappointment Condé appeared to care more for Charlotte than he did for hunting, for the young Prince, fearing the worst, asked Henry's permission to leave the court and take his wife with him. The King refused to give it and threatened him with dire consequences if he disobeyed.

Condé, however, left the Louvre with his wife and went to the Château de Valery, where he received an order from the King to return immediately and was told that if he did not the marriage would be annulled and the princess brought to the Louvre and kept there. On 29th November, therefore, Condé 'abducted' his wife, crossed the frontier into the Low Countries and put himself under the protection of the Arch-duke Albert and his wife, who ruled there under the Sovereignty of the King of Spain.

Henry learned of their escape on the same day and wasted no time. He sent the Chevalier du Get* in pursuit of the fugitives and demanded that the Archduke should have Condé and Charlotte sent back to France at once. The Archduke was in some difficulty. He did not see how he could decently hand over a prince of the blood who had asked for asylum, nor did he want to offend the King of France. Never-theless he promised to do all in his power to persuade the runaway couple to return. That did not satisfy Henry, who insisted that Condé and Charlotte be repatriated to France immediately. Meanwhile the Spaniards attached to the Archduke's Court – led by Spinola†, who had himself taken a fancy to the princess – took advantage of the situation. Spinola told the Prince de Condé that as one of the princes of the blood he should insist on his rights and even contest the validity of the King's second marriage. Condé refused to take

* Literally, the Knight of the Watch. His duties *vis a vis* the King were somewhat similar to the Special Branch of Scotland Yard.
† Spinola was Commander-in-Chief of the Spanish Army in the Low Countries.

Spinola's advice but, nevertheless, decided to seek refuge in Milan, leaving his wife in Brussels under the care of the Archduchess.

This did not make the Archduke's task any easier. It had never been Condé whom the King wanted back in Paris but Charlotte, and she was still in Brussels under the Archduke's jurisdiction. Henry had even tried to have her kidnapped and had forced Montmorency to demand the return of his daughter, but the Archduke had said that he could only extradite her if her husband requested it, unless, of course, the couple were either divorced or the marriage annulled.

Meanwhile Charlotte was bored to tears. She did not really love her husband, to whom she had only been married because, as Henry had said, he wanted "to keep her in the family." She also missed the gay life at the Louvre. She had remained in touch with the King, who wrote to her frequently and sent her presents. Madame Berry, the wife of the French Ambassador in Brussels never ceased singing the praises of her royal lover, and all Charlotte really wanted was to return to the Louvre, even if it meant that she would have to be the King's mistress.

Henry's passion for Charlotte had reached such a stage that he was prepared to go to war in order to get her back to Paris. By the early spring of 1610 the plans for putting the 'Grand Design' into execution had nearly reached completion. He was already sure that England would support him, and he knew that he could count on the Protestant princes of Germany. The Kings of Sweden and Denmark had also promised their assistance, and the Duke of Bavaria had also agreed to join the alliance provided he became the King of Rome. Even the Pope was attracted by the fact that the 'Grand Design' might lead to the Kingdom of Naples being reunited with the Holy See.

The army had been put on a war footing, and Sully had succeeded in amassing the necessary financial resources and adequate stocks of ammunition and supplies to open the campaign. La Force, who had been appointed Maréchal de France was ready as soon as the word was given to invade Spain with an army of 50,000, and Lesdiguieres would then cross the Alps with a force of 20,000 to join up with the Duc de Savoie, who had also agreed to take part in the enterprise on condition that his son would be married to Henry IV's eldest legitimate daughter. All that was needed was a plausible pretext for going to war, and it was not long before this was forthcoming.

It was the dispute over the succession of the duchies of Cleves-Julich. Had Henry given armed support to the claim of the natural heirs of the Duchy of Cleves against the Elector of Saxony a general war would have broken out in 1610 and that was exactly what he wanted and would have got but for his assassination.

However, he decided that before he went to war he must have the Queen formally crowned. In order to ensure that the government of France would go on as before during his absence, which might be quite a long one, he had appointed Marie de Medici Regent.

Before the end of 1609 there was a tense atmosphere in Paris and a general feeling that something was going to happen, for a rumour had gone round the city that the Huguenots were planning a St Bartholomew massacre of Catholics to take place on Christmas Day, and that the King knew of the plot and had not dared to do anything to stop it.

Included in the many people who believed it, was an ardent Catholic from Angoulême named François Ravaillac, who was about 32 years of age. He had had a varied career, having been first of all the valet of a judge and later a schoolmaster. He had also been in a debtor's prison, during which time he was troubled with visions, and he had become extremely unbalanced. After he had served his sentence he wanted to see the King in order to tell him that he should either ban the Huguenots or force them to become Catholics, and he approached Cardinal du Perron and asked him to apply for an audience with His Majesty.

On 27th December 1609 Ravaillac was amongst the crowd watching the King driving through Paris, and as he passed by Ravaillac shouted, "Sire, in the name of Our Lord Jesus Christ and the Virgin Mary, may I speak to you," but the troops who were guarding the route pushed him back into the crowd and he returned to Angoulême.

While he was there someone told him that the King was

taking up arms on behalf of the Protestants in Germany and
that the Pope's Ambassador in Paris had said that if the King
made war against His Holiness he (the Ambassador) would
have Henry excommunicated, to which the King replied
that his predecessors had put the Popes on their thrones and
if he were excommunicated he would depose them.

All these stories and rumours had affected Ravaillac's
unbalanced mind to such an extent that he decided to kill
the King, and he returned to Paris in April 1610, only to be
told by some of the King's troops, to whom he had spoken,
that if Henry declared war on the Pope they would fight with
him and be only too willing to die in such a holy cause. This
was the last straw, for Ravaillac considered that to make
war on the Pope was sacrilege for, as he said, "The Pope is
God, and God is the Pope."

Shortly after his return to Paris Ravaillac stole a knife
from a hostelry which he hid in one of his pockets and carried
about with him for three weeks, waiting for an opportunity
to carry out his divine mission, but somehow or other he could
not bring himself to do it, and he decided once again to return
to Angouleme.

On his way there, however, he passed a crucifix outside
Etampes, and as he saw the figure of Jesus Christ on the
cross crowned with thorns it seemed to reproach him for his
lack of courage and unfaithfulness. He turned back without
hesitation and arrived in Paris shortly before the Queen's
coronation which was due to take place on 13th May.

For some time the soothsayers and astrologers had been
predicting the death of the King, and he himself had a presentiment that his end was not far off. Only a few days before
the coronation he said to Sully, "I shall die in this city and
shall never get away from it. . . . They will kill me for there
is no way out of their danger except by my death." He had
also told Bassompierre that he was sure he would never get to
Germany and believed that he would soon be dead. It was
not because he paid any attention to the soothsayers and
astrologists that he had fears but because of the reports he had
received from his police that Paris was seething with unrest.
He had told some of his courtiers that they were mad to
believe all these prognostications. "For thirty years," he told

them, "these astrologers have been predicting my death each year."

The date predicted for the King's assassination was 14th May, the day after the Queen's coronation, and he had already decided to leave Paris on 17th to join his troops, who were assembling near Chalons before marching to the Low Countries.

On 14th May the King left the Louvre in the royal coach, taking with him the Duc d'Epernon and two or three members of his suite, to go to the Arsenal to talk to Sully. In the rue de la Ferronerie, which was very narrow, they were held up by a traffic block.

Since early morning Ravaillac had been keeping watch on the gates of the Louvre and had followed the King. While the coach was still held up by the traffic he managed to get close to the King, who was sitting with his hand on the shoulder of Epernon, who was reading a letter to him. Ravaillac stabbed the King, who cried out, "I am wounded," and was immediately stabbed a second time. Henry murmured, "It is nothing," but blood was gushing out of his mouth.

The assassin made no attempt whatsoever to escape, but stood there, his knife still in his hand. When an officer of the King's guard drew his sword and rushed towards Ravaillac, Epernon at the risk of his own life, prevented the officer from killing him.

Ravaillac was arrested and taken to the Hotel de Retz, only a short distance away, where he was guarded by the King's archers. Epernon then told the crowd that His Majesty was only wounded. But he appeared to be already dead. Whether he was, in fact, dead or whether he died on the way to the Louvre has never been definitely established, but as soon as he arrived there he was taken to a small room adjoining the royal apartment, where attempts were made to revive him with a few drops of wine. The King's physician, however, is reported to have said that the King opened his eyes two or three times when exhorted to commend his soul to God.

The Queen was immediately sent for, but by the time she arrived with the Dauphin Henry no longer showed any sign of life. The Queen, who had spent most of her married life quarreling with her husband, admittedly not without some

reason, completely lost control of herself, and her cries were
heard all over the palace. When she said "The King is dead.
The King is dead," Sully, who had arrived a few minutes
earlier, told her that in France Kings never died and pointing
to the young Dauphin said, "Madame, there is the living King".
He also rather heartlessly advised her to keep her tears for a
better occasion.

The news of the King's assassination spread round the city
like wildfire, and the Parisians were stunned with grief. All
the shops closed, and the people gathered together in little
groups at every street corner, giving each other the latest
news and demanding vengeance against the instigators of the
plot to kill the King, for they knew he had many enemies in
high places and refused to believe that his assassination was
just the work of a madman.   •

In Paris during the last few months Henry had begun to
lose some of his popularity due mainly to the heavy increase
in taxation, the scandals of the court, which were common
knowledge, and the threat of another war; but in an instant
all these had been forgotten and the King was remembered
as a man who loved his subjects and had brought France
better times. And what a change there had been between the
Treaty of Vervins in 1598 and the end of his reign. Order had
been re-established in the country's economy and administration, and hope for the future had been restored. Without
going to war Henry IV had helped Holland to free herself
of the Spanish invaders and revived the authority of France
in Europe.

In the provinces of France the news of the King's death
caused even more consternation than it had done in the capital.

> It was pitiful to see [wrote Mathieu*] throughout all the provinces
> the poor people from the villages standing in large groups along
> the main roads looking haggard and perplexed to find out from
> passers by what had really happened and when they had been
> told all the details going back one by one to their homes like sheep
> without a shepherd.

Another graphic account of the people's distress and morti-
fication was given to Louis XIV by Bossuet† sixty years later.

* A historian of the seventeenth century.
† A bishop and historian.

At the time of Henry's death one could see, not only throughout the whole country but in every family, in addition to astonishment, horror and indignation at the execrable deed, a deep sense of bereavement such as that which children experience on the death of a good kind father. There is not one of us who has not heard his grandfather or father talk of the kindness of this great King to his people and the extreme love of the people for him.

The King's remains, embalmed and clothed in white satin, lay in state in the large reception hall at the Louvre until his body was placed in the coffin; and all the people of Paris filed past in reverent silence, while a hundred masses were said each day in Notre Dame and all the parish churches. All the leading bishops in relays prayed constantly at the foot of the catafalque, and on 25th June the young King, Louis XIII sprinkled it with holy water. The funeral service was held at St Denis with great pomp and ceremony, and all the houses and buildings in the streets through which the funeral procession passed were draped with black cloth, and candles were burning in all the windows. The crowds were so dense that it was hardly possible for most of them to see the cortège.*

The King's body was buried in the vault of St Denis and remained there until the French Revolution, when, in 1793, the *sans-culottes*† ransacked the abbey and disinterred and mutilated what remained of all the kings of France and other famous Frenchmen who had been buried there. According to contemporary accounts of what were called the 'desecrations' – for they were not confined to the abbey of St Denis – the embalmed body of Henry IV was in a remarkable state of preservation. The sans-culottes attached it to one of the pillars on the west façade of the abbey church, where it was left to the mercy of the populace. His moustache was cut off, his skull sawn in pieces, his bones thrown into the gutter.

Revolutionary France may have had good reason to detest the Bourbons, but she had obviously forgotten, did not know, or did not want to know what the first of them had done for his country and, above all for his people nearly two centuries earlier.

So many legends about the early days of Henry IV have

* See *Henry IV* by Maurice Andrieux, p. 499.
† Violent Republicans.

been handed down to posterity that the following account of
a strange happening in Pau the night before he was assassinated
would certainly be dismissed as being just one more fairy story
had it not been described in the *Memoirs* of La Force, who
was the Commander-in-Chief of the French army in 1610
and was with the King in the royal coach at the time of his
assassination. But as Byron wrote in *Don Juan*:*

> Tis strange but true; for truth is always strange, –
> Stranger than fiction.

A remarkable thing happened in the Béarn [La Force wrote] on
the eve of the King's death. To understand it better one has to
know that the coat of arms of the province of Béarn consists of two
cows, because at the beginning of May all the cows in that part of
France are taken to the foothills and mountains around Pau. On
the night of 13th/14th May 1610 a large herd of cattle, mooing
and bellowing, entered the suburbs of Pau and the town itself.
They went as far as the small bridge which spans the moat
surrounding the Château de Pau, which was the cradle of the
great King Henry, where they continued mooing and bellowing
louder than ever which astounded the inhabitants. While this was
going on the only bull in the whole herd jumped over the bridge
into the moat where it was found dead next morning. All the cows
then went away bellowing in a most frightening manner.

On 27th May Ravaillac was quartered in the Place de Greve
in Paris in the presence of many thousands of people each of
whom could have wished for nothing better than to have been
the executioner. His remains were then literally torn to pieces
by the crowd and trodden under foot. Many of the spectators
were sorry that Ravaillac was the only person executed, for
they were convinced that the assassination of Henry IV was
not just the act of a madman but the result of a conspiracy
in which persons of high repute were involved.

The inquest on the King's murder has continued ever since,
and while it is impossible to say with any certainty who the
conspirators were, there now seems little if any doubt that
Ravaillac, although it was he who delivered the fatal blow,
was only the instrument used by others who wanted to get
rid of the King.

* Canto, XIV, stanza 101.

18 The inquest

AMONG those who never doubted that the assassination of Henry IV was the result of a conspiracy was Achille de Harlay, a leading Huguenot, who had been imprisoned in the Bastille by Henry III and released immediately after Henry IV's accession to the throne in 1589. In 1610 he was the First President of the Parlement of Paris, and when asked what evidence he had to support his suspicions he said, "I have plenty."

The most recent and thorough investigation of the evidence has been made by Philippe Erlanger, who summarized it in a book entitled *L'Etrange Mort de Henri IV*.

There were many people who wanted to get rid of the King and were prepared to go to almost any length to achieve it, and there were many more who would welcome his death, even though they might not be prepared to become involved in it.

Among the former were the Duc d'Epernon and his mistress, Madame du Tillet; the Duc d'Auvergne; the Duc de Bouillon; Henriette d'Entragues, and her father; Concini, whom Marie de Medici had brought with her from Italy before her marriage to the King; and the Jesuits.

Ravaillac when interrogated by the three magistrates whom Achille de Harlay had appointed to investigate the murder, however, protested that he had acted quite independently and that he regarded the assassination of the King as a 'divine mission' for which he would be given credit in the hereafter. Even a little torture – he had his thumbs crushed – produced no effect, and he still refused to incriminate anyone. Two bishops tried to get him to tell the truth before his execution by promising him absolution, but with no avail. He was also seen, while he was still at the Hotel de Retz, by several Jesuit fathers, one of whom was rash enough to tell him that on no account must he accuse anyone of importance. The Jesuits were, of course, well aware that they were under suspicion because of their involvement in the attempted assassination of Henry IV by Chastel which led to their banishment from France.

Of all the suspects Epernon was probably at the top of the list. To begin with he had known Ravaillac for some time and had he wanted to find someone to assassinate the King he could not have chosen anyone more suitable than a crazy fanatic who conceived that by so doing he was furthering God's will. Furthermore Ravaillac had not been secretive about his ambition. He had spoken of it to many people, and it is more than likely that Epernon had learned of this. He had also been involved, according to evidence which is now available, in both the Biron and Entragues conspiracies, and his hatred for Henry was no secret. He had been one of Henry III's 'little darlings'* and ever since the submission of The League had been in conflict with the King. Nor was this all. There were three other things which seemed highly suspicious.

Firstly, it had not escaped the notice of some of the eye-witnesses of the murder that, after the first blow had been struck, Epernon had made no attempt, as he could easily have done, to protect the King against further violence.

Secondly, while Ravaillac was still at the Hotel de Retz Epernon managed to take him to his own house, where he remained all day. What went on during that time behind those closed doors nobody knows, but many people thought that if he remained at the Retz he might be forced or persuaded to tell the truth, as it would have made no difference to his ultimate fate for he was bound to be executed in any event. This might have been mere guesswork, but there was some evidence to support it, although it was purely circumstantial.

Thirdly, Epernon threatened to stab one of the magistrates appointed to investigate the crime unless he undertook not to inquire into the role which he or the Queen had played in the affair – for even she was under some suspicion, not of having

* See page 45.

been directly involved in a conspiracy but of having known about its existence and turning a blind eye.

During the last few years of her married life she had been afraid of her husband who had already threatened to send her back to Italy, and she even suspected that he might take take her life. This presentiment was so strong that she refused to eat or drink anything that came from Henry's table lest it should contain poison.

The assassination of the King was also in Concini's interest for he was Marie de Medici's right-hand man and when she became Regent he would have considerable influence over her – the sooner the better. Concini was married to Leonora Galigaï, the Queen's personal maid, who was later appointed Mistress of the Robes and shared all her innermost thoughts. The influence of this couple, which, while Henry was alive, was so strong that it made him both furious and jealous, became even greater after his death. The Queen Regent gave them both a handsome allowance, and she made Concini Marquis d'Ancre and governor of Peronne, Roye and Montdidier. He had also been for many years a secret agent in the service of Spain and had been passing on valuable secret information which Henry had from time to time confided to his wife in unguarded moments.

There appeared to be no real evidence implicating either Bouillon or Auvergne in any plot to assassinate the King, but they had both been involved in the Biron and Entragues conspiracies and might have been prepared to plot another attempt on his life provided they could be certain that this time it would be successful.

There was another aspect of the case, however, which convinced many people that everything was being done to keep the whole business under the carpet.

Was there not, perhaps, another conspiracy, the object of which was not to enquire too deeply into the assassination. For had it been discovered that it was the work of the Jesuits, the former chiefs of The League or one of the people who had previously conspired against the King – such as Auvergne, Entragues or Bouillon – the whole country would be involved in bloodshed. This suspicion was heightened by the fact that the investigation was held *in camera*, and none of the evidence

given was ever published. The greater part of the inquiry was
taken up with the personal motives which prompted Ravaillac
to kill the King. The commission of inquiry were perfectly
aware that there was evidence that other persons were involved,
but, apart from interrogating a number of high-ranking
Jesuits, they purposely avoided, or so it would seem, calling
any witnesses whose names had been mentioned by Jacqueline
Escoman*. It is not surprising, therefore, that when a fire
broke out in the Louvre in 1618 many people thought that
it was not accidental but that it had been done purposely to
destroy the documents relating to the trial of Ravaillac and
Escoman† which were kept in the palace archives.

All the above considerations make it extremely difficult to
avoid coming to the conclusion that there was something to
hide and that the best way to do so was to attribute the
assassination of the King to Ravaillac's 'divine mission'. It
was not difficult to do this because Ravaillac's background
made it quite plausible. He was a native of Angoulême, a
city which had suffered greatly during the religious wars,
and his two uncles who were both canons in the diocese had
brought him up to hate the 'heretics' of the Reformed Churches.
It was not, however, necessarily a coincidence that Epernon
was the governor of Angoulême, and it is more than probable
that he knew all about Ravaillac's extreme views, particularly
as Epernon's hatred of the King was generally known.

Another aspect of the case which required an explanation
that was never forthcoming was the fact that in Spain and the
Low Countries the news that the King had been assassinated
was announced some eight days before it took place, and on
the 9th of May a soldier advised a Protestant friend who lived
in Paris to leave the city as quickly as possible as something
was shortly going to happen which might lead to severe
measures being taken against the members of the Reformed
Churches. Furthermore, the Provost of Pithiviers, who was
in the pay of the Entragues, actually announced the murder
of the King while it was taking place, and why was it that
shortly afterwards he was strangled in prison?

In a biography of 'Henry the Great' written in 1661,

* See page 191.
† See page 194.

Hardouin de Perefixe summed up the position as follows:

> There is no doubt whatsover that there were many conspiracies
> against the life of this good king, but if one asks who were the
> Demons and the Furies who put it into execution the answer of
> History is that their names are not known and that in such an
> important matter one should not regard suspicions and conjec-
> tures as positive proof.

He might, however, have added these words: "unless corroborated by reliable independent evidence."

It is true that the evidence of the motives which a number
of people had for getting rid of Henry IV and of the fact that
some of them had previously been involved in conspiracies
to take his life amounted to no more than suspicion without
corroboration, and it is for that reason that the evidence
given by Jacqueline d'Escoman was of such importance, and
if the magistrates did not consider it was reliable enough to
corroborate the other evidence why was it that she was sentenced to life imprisonment in respect of another charge which
had nothing whatsoever to do with the case.

Jacqueline d'Escoman, née Le Voyer, was married to a
man who ill-treated her abominably and lived on her immoral
earnings until he eventually deserted her and left her with a
child and no money. She left the baby in charge of a wet
nurse and started looking for employment on the domestic
staff of a member of the aristocracy. She obtained an intro-
duction to Marguerite de Valois, who, after making enquiries
into her previous history, did not engage her. She was then
taken on the staff of the Marquise de Verneuil's sister, Marie
d'Entragues, who afterwards passed her on to Henriette, and
it was in this way that she became involved in the Ravaillac
inquiry which was to end so disastrously for her.

While she was with Henriette d'Entragues, she became her
personal maid, and she learned many things which disturbed
her greatly. On one occasion she overheard a conversation
between the Duc d'Epernon and Henriette which left her in
no doubt that they were both involved in a conspiracy to
assassinate the King. She also noticed that Henriette had
many visitors at her house who, although they looked like
Frenchmen, she felt certain were not. Later she had good

reason to believe that they were Spanish. She also saw Mademoiselle du Tillet, Epernon's mistress, and discovered that Ravaillac had been to her house on many occasions and that she had given him money.

Hearing that a messenger was shortly leaving Henriette's house to go to Spain carrying with him important documents, Escoman decided that something must be done, and she made several attempts to see the Queen but without success. On each occasion she was asked to come back in a few days' time, but when she returned she was told that unfortunately the Queen had suddenly had to go away.

After three or four such attempts she returned to Mademoiselle du Tillet who had recently taken her on as lady's maid. For some time she did nothing more until she suddenly decided to go and see the Jesuits and tell them everything she knew. If she had only stopped to think, however, she would have realized they were the last people she should have approached, and it may not have surprised her when the Père Procureur* of the Jesuits, with whom she managed to obtain an interview, after hearing what she had to say, told her "go away and pray to God."

For a long time she wondered what to do next and suddenly conceived the brilliant idea of telling the whole story to Mademoiselle de Gournay, whom she had heard spoken of as an intelligent and reliable woman and whom she happened to know was a great admirer of Henry IV as a king, although she did not approve of his private life.

One evening when the Comte de Schomberg† was dining with Sully at the Arsenal a messenger arrived with a short note from Mademoiselle de Gournay saying that she wished to see him urgently on a matter of great importance. He went to see her immediately, and she repeated what Escomant had told her. Schomberg did not know whether to believe it or not. On the other hand it might be nothing more than idle gossip for it would not be the first time there had been an attempt on the King's life; on the other hand he knew that Mademoiselle de Gournay would not have told him unless

* The senior Father.

† Gaspard de Schomberg, a naturalized Frenchman, at one time Governor of the Marche province.

she had checked it carefully. He therefore decided to ask Sully's advice before taking any action, thinking that Sully would at once take some steps to have Escoman's story investigated and, at the same time, warn the King – but he did neither.

In his *Memoirs* Sully gave his reasons for deciding to do nothing:

> The matter was too important to take no notice of it but if I had told the King it would have resulted in all those whose names had been mentioned as being involved in the plot becoming my implacable enemies. Schomberg and I agreed that he should speak to the King about it with as much discretion as possible and that if His Majesty demanded to know the names of the conspirators he should be advised to interview Escoman and Gournay and find out the facts from them.

What would have happened next had not fate intervened it is impossible to guess, but Jacqueline d'Escoman was arrested for abandoning her child on the Pont-Neuf. She did so because the woman who had charge of the child was owed a lot of money and told Escoman that she must either pay up or take back the child. She was taken to the Conciergerie and later tried and sent to prison. Although the offence of abandoning a child was punishable in the seventeenth century with a sentence of death, it is most unlikely that Jacqueline d'Escoman would have been sentenced to imprisonment for life had she not become an embarrassment to the 'establishment', and it should not be forgotten that Marie de Medici was now the Regent. Since it had become known that Escoman was in possession of evidence which might have incriminated a number of very important people, all her movements had obviously been closedly watched, otherwise it is most improbable that she would have been arrested within a few hours of her leaving her child on the Pont-Neuf.

When she appealed against her sentence she was released and allowed to go and live in a convent chosen for the purpose by the Court of Appeal. As she was allowed a certain amount of freedom she managed to obtain an interview with Marguerite de Valois in 1611, when she told the ex-Queen all she knew about the Duc d'Epernon, the Marquise de Verneuil and Mademoiselle du Tillet being involved in a plot to assassinate the King.

N

What happened after the interview was set out in a report made by the Venetian Ambassador in Paris:

Escoman told Marguerite de Valois that a long time before he killed the King Ravaillac used to pay frequent visits to Mademoiselle du Tillet and that Henriette d'Entragues' reason for wishing the King out of the way was that she hoped to marry the Duc de Guise and then be proclaimed Regent while Epernon was to be rewarded by being appointed Constable of France in succession to Montmorency.

Two days later, having been asked by Marguerite de Valois to come back and see her, Escoman was arrested a second time and taken to the Conciergerie for further interrogation. She repeated what she had told Marguerite de Valois about Mademoiselle du Tillet and Ravaillac, but this time her evidence was corroborated by a *valet de chambre* who said that he had seen Ravaillac there. Later Henriette d'Entragues was also summoned to the Conciergerie and examined for five hours, but what happened during her interrogation is not known.

Was Jacqueline d'Escoman's evidence reliable or was it not? As no record of it is extant, it is impossible to judge. Nevertheless she does not appear to have had any ulterior motive for fabricating her story and she had undoubtedly been in a position to have heard and seen everything which she described.

It is difficult to avoid the conclusion that the whole truth about the assassination was deliberately suppressed. Philippe Erlanger has likened the murder of Henry IV to the burning of the Reichstag in Berlin in 1933, Goering corresponding to Epernon, and von Lubbe to Ravaillac.

HENRY THE GREAT

HENRY IV has been known ever since his reign as Henri *le Grand*. He was also known as the *Vert Galant*, which can best be translated as 'the dashing ladies' man', and that he certainly was. But his private life in no way affected his competence to govern France, which he did with foresight, good judgment and in the interest of his people, which he placed before anything else.

It should not be forgotten that a scandal which in these days might rock the throne of any country was of little consequence in the sixteenth and seventeenth centuries. Henry was not the first or last European King to have several mistresses and it is not on that basis that he should be judged. It has even been suggested that some of his mistresses played a useful role. André Maurois in his *History of France* wrote:

> We may well wonder whether the King's mistresses, so damned by the historians, did not play an essential role by supplying, next to an all too-flattered sovereign, women who dared to speak to him as a human being. The privacy of the bedroom has a healthy levelling effect upon rank and dignity.

There is a great deal in what André Maurois has said. A few home truths do nobody any harm, and Henry's two favourite mistresses, Corisande and Gabrielle d'Estrées, were both intelligent and well-informed women. It is clear from some of the letters which he wrote to them that they both took an interest in what was going on, which was more than either of his wives did. They spent most of their time having rows with him and, as he once told Sully, Marie de Medici, whenever he tried to talk about anything interesting, immediately changed the subject. Be that as it may, ten generations of Frenchmen, and who should know better, have confirmed the judgment that Henry IV was a great king and one of France's national heroes.

CHRONOLOGY OF THE LIFE AND REIGN OF HENRY IV

1553   Birth of Henri de Bourbon at the Château de Pau (13th December).

1554   Catholic Baptism of the young prince in the large reception room in the Château de Pau (6th March).

1555   Death of Henri d'Albret, king of Navarre, grandfather of Henry IV (24th May). The prince is entrusted to the care of Suzanne de Bourbon-Busset, wife of Jean d'Albret, Baron de Miossens, to be brought up at the Chateau de Coarraze.

1557   February. First journey of Henri de Bourbon to the Court of France. He is presented to King Henry II and to his cousin Marguerite de Valois, whom he married in 1572

1559   Treaty of Cateau-Cambresis (April).
Accidental death of Henry II (10th July).
Accession of Francis II.
Francis, Duc de Guise and the Cardinal de Lorraine, uncles of the new king, are put at the head of the Government.
The Prince of Navarre begins his instruction in the Protestant faith. La Gaucherie is appointed as his tutor.

1560   The death of Francis II and the accession of Charles IX (5th December). Jeanne d'Albret publicly takes Communion (25th December).

1561   Antoine de Bourbon (Henry IV's father) is made Lieutenant-General of the Kingdom (27th March).
Jeanne d'Albret and her son arrive at the Court of France (July).

1562   Jeanne d'Albret leaves the Court. Her son, whom she had to leave there, is placed under the tutorship of Jean de Losse in order to bring him back to Catholicism. Taken to Mass by his father, he takes the oath to observe the Orthodox faith (1st June).

Antoine de Bourbon dies as the result of wounds during the siege of Rouen (17th November).

1563　His mother decides that the prince is to be brought up in the Calvinist religion.

1564　The Prince of Navarre accompanies Charles IX and Catherine de Medici on a long journey through the Kingdom.

Nostradamus predicts that the prince will become King of France (17th October).

1567　Jeanne d'Albret leaves the court with her son and returns to Pau. The prince becomes Lieutenant-General of the Kingdom of Navarre and has his first encounters with the Basque nobility.

1568　The Queen of Navarre takes her son to La Rochelle and hands him over to her brother-in-law, Louis de Bourbon, Prince de Condé, head of the Protestant army (September).

1569–1570　The campaigns of the prince, first under Condé and then Admiral de Coligny.

The battle of Jarnac (13th March 1569) and of Moncontour (3rd October).

The Treaty of Saint-Germain (August 1570).

1571　Sojourn of the Prince de Navarre in the Béarn.

Unsuccessful attempts made by Catherine de Medici to tempt him to return to the Louvre.

1572　Jeanne d'Albret dies (9th June).

Henry of Navarre becomes King of Navarre. He marries Marguerite de Valois (18th August).

1573–1575　The King of Navarre goes to the Louvre and stays there. The first years of his married life.

The siege of La Rochelle.

Henry after being forced to abjure the Protestant religion endeavours to explain his thoughts and political intentions to his Huguenot supporters.

Charles IX dies on 31st May 1574

Accession of Henry III.

1576　The King of Navarre leaves the court and returns to the practice of the Protestant religion.

Treaty of Beaulieu (6th May).

The power of 'The League'.

Henry of Navarre is appointed Governor of the Guyenne.

1577　Another religious war is ended by the Treaty of Bergerac (15th September).

1578   After thirty-two months of separation, Marguerite de Valois
       rejoins her husband at Nerac.
       Visit of Catherine de Medici to Nérac.

1579   Henry's Court at Nerac.

1580   The 'Lovers War'.
       The Treaty of Fleix (26th November).

1581   The return of Court life at Nerac.
       The affair of the King of Navarre and La Fosseuse.
       La Fosseuse gives birth to a child.

1582   Marguerite de Valois leaves for the Court of France (March).

1583   Corisande d'Andoin becomes Henry's mistress.
       Marguerite is banned from the Court by her brother Henry
       III under the pretext of her misbehaviour.

1584   Death of François de Valois, the Duc d'Anjou fourth son
       of Henry II (10th June).

1585   Marguerite settles in Agen under the pretext of safeguarding
       herself against the plots of Corisande to take her life. She
       is forced to take refuge in the Chateau d'Usson (March).
       Pope Sixtus V excommunicates Henry of Navarre and
       declares him unworthy of the crown of France (September).

1586   The war of the three Henrys (Henry III, Henry King of
       Navarre and Henri the Duc de Guise) begins.
       The King of Navarre leaves his government in the Guyenne
       to establish a base in the Saintonge for future operations.
       He arrives at La Rochelle (1st June).

1587   The battle of Coutras. Henry of Navarre fails to exploit
       his victory and returns to the Béarn (20th October).

1588   The Prince of Condé's death (5th March).
       Attempts against the life of the King of Navarre.
       Disturbances in Paris.
       Flight of Henry III.
       The Etats de Blois.
       Murder of the Duc de Guise (23rd December).

1589   Catherine de Medici dies (5th January).
       Reconciliation between Henry III and the King of Navarre.
       Interview of Plessis-les-Tours (30th April).
       The siege of Paris.
       Assassination of Henry III.
       Henry of Navarre becomes King of France (20th August).
       The battle of Arques (21st September).

1590   The battle of Ivry (14th March).
       The second siege of Paris (mid-September).

1591 The beginning of the King's liaison with Gabrielle d'Estrées.
   The siege of Rouen (December).

1592 The battle of Aumale (5th February).
   Defeats of the royal armies.

1593 The inauguration of the Etats Généraux of Paris (26th January).
   Henry IV abjures the Protestant religion (21st July).

1594 Coronation of the King (27th February).
   The King's entry into Paris (22nd March).
   Joining up of the great Leaguers.
   Attempts by Jean Chastel on the King's life (27th December).

1595 Banishment of the Jesuits (January).
   Declaration of war against Spain (17th January).
   The battle of Fontaine-Française (5th June).
   The Pope lifts the excommunication from the King (18th September).

1596 The siege of La Fère.

1597 Surprise attack on Amiens (12th March).
   The siege and capture of the city (25th September).

1598 The King signs the Edict of Nantes (13th April).
   The Treaty of Vervins (2nd May).
   The Duc de Mercoeur's submission to the King.

1599 Death of Gabrielle d'Estrées (10th April).
   The start of a liaison between the King and Henriette d'Entragues, Marquise de Verneuil.
   Engagement of the King to Marie de Medici.

1600 The campaign in Savoie.
   The King's second marriage.

1601 Presentation to the Queen of Henriette d'Entragues (9th February).
   Birth of the Dauphin, Louis (27th September).
   Bith of Henri (later Duc de Verneuil) (4th November).
   Many affaires of the King during the pregnancies of the Queen and his favourite mistress, Henriette.

1602 Conspiracy and execution of Biron (21st July).

1603 Serious illness of the King.
   Reconciliation between the Queen and the Marquise de Verneuil.
   Recall of the Jesuits (1st September).

1604 Serious family discords.
   Jacqueline de Bueil becomes the King's mistress.
   Discovery of the Entragues conspiracy.

1605   Trial, conviction and reprieve of the conspirators.
       Break with Henriette d'Entragues.
       Return of Marguerite de Valois to Paris.
1606   The Duc de Bouillon comes to terms with the King.
       Henriette d'Entragues is forgiven and returns to the Louvre.
1607   The King's liaison with Charlotte des Essarts.
1608   Another break with Henriette d'Entragues.
       The Spanish marriages affair.
1609   The last amour of the King (Charlotte de Montmorency).
       The Duc de Condé leaves the Louvre with her and asks for
       asylum in Brussels.
       The 'Grand Design'.
1610   The Queen's coronation (13th May).
       Henry IV is assassinated by François Ravaillac (14th May).

SHORT BIBLIOGRAPHY

Andrieux, Maurice	*Henri IV*
Aubigné, d'	*Mémoires*
Aumale, Duc d'	*Histoire des Princes de Condé*
Bassonpierre, Maréchal de	*Journal de ma vie*
Cheverny, Philippe Comte de	*Les mémoires d'Estat*
Elbée, Jean d'	*Le miracle de Henri IV*
Erlanger, Philippe	*L'Etrange mort de Henri IV*
	Le massacre de la St Barthelémy
Fisher, H. A. L.	*History of Europe*
La Force, Maréchal de	*Mémoires*
Lavisse, E.	*Histoire de France*
Lescure de	*Les amours de Henri IV*
L'Estoile	*Mémoires Journaux du règne de Henri IV*
Loiseleur	*Ravaillac et ses complices*
Matthieu, Pierre	*Histoire de la mort déplorable de Henri IV*
Maurois, André	*History of France*
Merki, Charles	*La Marquise de Verneuil et la mort de Henri IV*
Prault, Laurent	*L'Esprit de Henri IV*
Reinhard, M.	*Henri IV ou la France Sauvée*
Ritter, Raymond	*Corisande d'Andouins*
	Henri IV, l'Enfant de la guerre et de l'amour
	Henri IV, L'Homme
Slocombe, Georges	*Henri IV*

Index